William T Dobson

History of the Bassandyne Bible

the first printed in Scotland - with notices of the early printers of Edinburgh

William T Dobson

History of the Bassandyne Bible
the first printed in Scotland - with notices of the early printers of Edinburgh

ISBN/EAN: 9783337100209

Printed in Europe, USA, Canada, Australia, Japan

Cover: Foto ©Lupo / pixelio.de

More available books at **www.hansebooks.com**

THE BASSANDYNE BIBLE.

Vignette from Title-page of Bassandyne Bible.

HISTORY OF THE
BASSANDYNE BIBLE

THE FIRST PRINTED IN SCOTLAND

WITH NOTICES OF

The Early Printers of Edinburgh

BY

WILLIAM T. DOBSON

AUTHOR OF
"LITERARY FRIVOLITIES," "POETICAL INGENUITIES,"
"ROYAL CHARACTERS OF SCOTT," ETC. ETC.

WITH FACSIMILES AND OTHER ILLUSTRATIONS

WILLIAM BLACKWOOD AND SONS
EDINBURGH AND LONDON
MDCCCLXXXVII

[All rights reserved]

Ballantyne Press
BALLANTYNE, HANSON AND CO.
EDINBURGH AND LONDON

PREFACE.

THE history and pedigree of books and their writers is no new attraction to the curious, as is evidenced by the numerous scholarly treatises on this branch of knowledge. There appears to be a kind of romantic interest attached to all that concerns rare old editions, and the story of their production is often the story, on the part of either printer or publisher, of perseverance and energy in overcoming no ordinary difficulties. These men seem frequently to have been carried forward by a genuine faith and enthusiasm in the prosecution of the work to which they had given themselves, devoting, as they did, much labour, thought, and anxiety to the accomplishment of their purpose. No doubt the early printers were hampered much by the ignorance and superstition of the common people of the time, to whom their work would appear very mysterious, and it would be long ere the feeling of awe resulting from the strange secrecy which brooded over the houses of the early printers could be shaken off.

Preface.

We cannot but feel amused if we endeavour to picture to our minds the consternation excited by the first printed Bibles exposed for sale. Conceive a meeting of two fat friars, both bibliophiles and connoisseurs in manuscripts, quite in raptures over the neat clean copies of the Vulgate which they have managed to secure at an obvious bargain from the German stranger. Each praises his own through all the forms of the superlative. At last the volumes are brought forth and diligently compared, when, to the amazement and horror of the two reverend fathers, they are found to be exact counterparts — neither can distinguish his own. They fear to touch the *Doppelgänger*—they fear to burn their fingers—there must evidently have been some fell sinister influence at work here; but then arises the question whether his Satanic majesty could endure the sight of the Word of Truth long enough to produce such exact copies.

Difficulties and trials and troubles certainly lay in the way of the early printers, yet it is astonishing, in examining old books, to see how soon after the introduction of the art all that was necessary to it was found out and developed in the way of "imposing," "registering," "signaturing," and the binding of the sheets of a book. So far as concerns these, we have not, in these days of much mechanical achievement, improved upon the methods of the early craftsmen, while the rapid production now generally aimed at must be, in a great measure, to the neglect of those finer features of the art so much cultivated and developed by them.

"A real study of our early printed books," says Mr. Blades in his "Life of Caxton," "brings with it a knowledge, more or less, of all the arts and sciences taught in the fifteenth and sixteenth centuries. In this lies one of its chief attractions to the bibliographer. The invention of printing gave new life to all branches of knowledge, and if we thoughtfully consider the wonderful effects which have proceeded from it—effects far more important to mankind than even the discovery of steam power, electric power, or any other invention—we shall surely feel deeply interested in all that concerns its introduction and spread in our country."

With a feeling akin to this the present writer has sought to give a brief account of some of the early printers of Edinburgh, and particularly of Thomas Bassandyne and the first Bible printed in Scotland, with the difficulties and impediments which lay in the way of its production. In connection with this, the little volume will be found to contain many curious and interesting things— things honest and of good report—things of historical and antiquarian interest and value—not readily accessible to ordinary readers, relating to the books and printers of Old Edinburgh. It was not thought, when the work was begun, that information regarding Thomas Bassandyne and his Bible would be so very difficult to procure; but only a few books of the many consulted proved to be of much service, and the information had to be gathered piecemeal, here a little and there a little, out of many outlying nooks and corners of our old literature. Histories of the period, and other books which were thought to be most likely to give contemporary side-views of local incidents, were almost absolutely barren in this direction, while even volumes treating of Typographical Antiquities, full enough in other respects, tell comparatively little about Bassandyne and his Bible. Even James Watson, an Edinburgh printer of the end of the seventeenth and beginning of the eighteenth centuries, gives no information, though he wrote one of the earliest works on the History of Printing—a book one would naturally have supposed to contain some notice of the old printer and his work.

Limited time and opportunities may well render this contribution to the socio-history of Edinburgh less complete than otherwise it might be, but the writer has conscientiously availed himself of every advantage within his reach, and where defects or omissions may be found, for these every apology is tendered. It is given to few to feel assured that every particular of a cherished object has been duly accomplished, and the present writer cannot say he is of that happy minority, and can only hope that this effort may lead some abler individual to follow suit in the composition of a fuller and more comprehensive work regarding the early printers of Edinburgh.

CONTENTS.

CHAPTER I.

Introduction of the Bible into Scotland . . . 17

The Reformation—Importation of Bibles—Patrick Hamilton—Henry Forrest—Alexander Ales—The Bible Prohibited—Secular Literature—Sir David Lyndsay—Cardinal Beaton—Scots Parliament of March 1543—Reading of the Bible Permitted—The Earl of Arran—Renewal of Persecution—George Wishart.

CHAPTER II.

Translations of the Bible 39

The Invention of Printing—Erasmus—William Tyndale—His New Testament—Bishop Tonstal—Burning the Bible—Martyrdom of Tyndale—Coverdale—Matthews' Bible—Taverner's Bible—The Great Bible—Prohibition of the Bible—Queen Mary of England—Bishop Bonner—John Bodley—The Geneva Version.

CHAPTER III.

Introduction of Printing into Edinburgh . . 69

James IV.—Andrew Myllar—Walter Chepman—The "Porteous of Noblenes"—The "Breviarium Aberdonense"—The Poet Dunbar—John Story—Thomas Davidson—

License to Print Acts of Parliament—John Scott—The "Complaynte of Scotland"—Hamilton's "Catechisme"—The "Twopenny Faith"—Restrictions on the Press—The "Tragedy of the Cardinal"—Niniane Winzet—Henrie Charteris—The General Assembly and the Printers—Robert Lekprevik—First License to Print the Bible—The "Donat"—Regent Morton—Satires against the Regent.

CHAPTER IV.

Bassandyne and Arbuthnot . 101

"Fall of the Roman Kirk"—Alexander Arbuthnot—Proposal to Print the Bible—Assent of the General Assembly—The "Corrector" and "Composer"—Impediments and Difficulties—Government License for Bible—Partnership Disputes—Publication of the Bible—The Dedicatory Epistle—Enforced Sale of the Bible—Arbuthnot appointed King's Printer—Thomas Vautrollier, a Huguenot Printer.

CHAPTER V.

The Bassandyne Bible 126

Collation—Size and Type—Title and Vignette—The Illustrations—The Genevan "Copy" used—The "Arguments" and Notes—King James the Sixth and the Genevan Notes—The Apocrypha—Tables and Indexes.

CHAPTER VI.

The Successors of Bassandyne . . . 158

Popular Books—"The Seven Sages"—George Young—Books Printed on the Continent—Andro Hart—Thomas Norton—Customs Duties on Books—Hart's Folio Bible—Napier's Logarithms—"Booke of Godlie and Spirituall Sangs"—Thomas Finlayson—Sir John Skene—"Regiam Majestatem"—Robert Young—The Archbishop of Canterbury's Bibles—The Scottish Service Book—Covenanting Troubles—Proclamations of Charles the First—"The Remonstrance of the Nobility," &c.

CHAPTER VII.

Evan Tyler—The Andersons 177

Evan Tyler—New Presbyterian Psalm Book—Archibald Hyslop—Andro Anderson—Monopoly of Printing—Robert Sanders—Sir Thomas Murray and the Statutes—Mrs. Anderson—Incorrect Bibles—Curious Blunders—"Satan's Invisible World Discovered"—The Lord Chancellor and the Bookseller—"The Root of Romish Ceremonies."

CHAPTER VIII.

Watson, Symson, and Ruddiman 194

James Watson—The Darien Riots—The Edinburgh Gazette—Captain Donaldson—The Courant—Adam Boig—Scottish Newspapers—Robert Freebairn—First History of Printing—Rebellion of 1715—Watson's Bibles—Andrew Symson—Thomas Ruddiman, Author and Printer—First Sale of Books by Auction—The Caledonian Mercury.

List of Authorities 221

Index 223

LIST OF ILLUSTRATIONS.

Vignette from Title of Bassandyne Bible	Frontispiece
Sir David Lyndsay	Page 33
First Page of Tyndale's Testament	43
Burning Bibles at Paul's Cross	51
The Chained Bible	61
Andrew Myllar's Device	77
Sixteenth Century Printing-Office	91
Bookbinding in Sixteenth Century	109
Paper-making in Sixteenth Century	113
Title of Bassandyne's New Testament	117
Initial from Tyndale's Testament	126
Facsimile page (reduced) of Bassandyne Bible	127
Garden of Eden, from Bassandyne Bible	135
The Ark, from Bassandyne Bible	143
Red Sea, from Bassandyne Bible	151
Initial from Bassandyne Bible	176
Title-page of Evan Tyler's Scotch Psalms for English Printed Bibles	179
Thomas Ruddiman	215

The Bassandyne Bible.

CHAPTER I.

Introduction of the Bible into Scotland.

THE doctrines of the Reformation, more especially those which asserted the supreme authority of the written Word and the independence of the individual conscience from all ecclesiastical domination, had made considerable progress in Scotland about 1525, aided latterly by the importation of some of Luther's writings. This greatly alarmed the clergy, to whom the name of the great Reformer was a word of terror, and they procured an Act of Parliament in 1525, requiring that "no manner of persons *strangers* that happened to arrive with their ships, within any part of the realm, should bring with them any books of the said Luther, his disciples, or servants, on pain of imprisonment, besides the forfeiture

forfeiture of their ships and goods." This edict seemingly failed to effect their purpose, and fresh alarm seized the clergy because of a rumour that the forbidden works were being brought into the country by the "king's lieges." In August 1527, accordingly, an additional clause was added to the former edict. "That all other, the king's lieges, assistaries to such opinions, be punished in seemable wise, and the effect of the said Act to strike upon them."

As the importation of "books of religion" was a clandestine and dangerous traffic, there is no distinct record of it, though little doubt exists that some of Luther's writings had entered Scotland by this time, but the only books which can be certainly traced were copies of Tyndale's New Testament. Not only was this the case in Scotland, but also in England—both countries being supplied from the Continent; and neither, though so closely connected, being in this matter dependent on the other. John Hackett was English ambassador in Antwerp at the time of this clandestine importation, and one of his duties was to purchase and burn, or "see justice done," to all such English books as were called the New Testament, "for the preservation of Christian faith." In a letter dated 20th February 1526, Hackett informed Cardinal Wolsey that "there were

were divers *merchants of Scotland* that bought many like books, and sent them from Zealand into Scotland; a part to Edinburgh, and more part to the town of St. Andrews." As February was the closing month of the year, which then began in March, it is evident, from the first edict referred to above, that these were not the first copies of Tyndale's New Testament brought into Scotland in that manner; as, besides St. Andrews, the ports of Leith, Montrose, and Aberdeen traded with Zealand. No official steps to exclude the Bible by name being taken for five years after this, it may reasonably be inferred that many copies entered again and again by those ports, and that the best part of them, as Hackett says, found their way to St. Andrews, "the very metropolis of superstition."

By the reception of the Bible into the country, the years 1525 and 1526 thus became, as has been well said, "by far the most remarkable in the annals of Scotland." The welcome the Book received, however, was not an unmixed one. The common people received it gladly, but its introduction met with fierce opposition from men in authority —alike from clergy, lawgivers and lawyers, and scholars, who deprecated its admission as an evil of the greatest magnitude; for they very soon realised

realised that, if the Scriptures once got possession of the minds of the people, their authority and influence would ultimately be undermined. One Scottish priest wrote against the common people having the Word of God in their own hands as follows: "Are all merchands, tailours, souters, baxters, wha cannot learne their awin craftes without skilful maisters, ar thir, I say, and uther temporal men, of whatsomever vocation or degree, sufficient doctor of thame selfis to reid and understand the hie mysteries of the Bible? What folie is it that wemen, wha cannot sew, cairde, nor spin, without they lerne the same of uther skilful wemen, suld usurp to reid and interpret the Bible!" About the same time, Dr. Buckenham, prior of Blackfriars, London, spoke at Cambridge in a similar strain of the danger of having the Scriptures in the native tongue: "If that heresy," said he, "should prevail, we should soon see an end of everything useful among us. The ploughman reading that if he put his hand to the plough, and should happen to look back, he was unfit for the kingdom of God, would soon lay aside his labour; the baker, likewise, reading that a little leaven will corrupt the whole lump, would give us very insipid bread; the simple man likewise finding himself commanded to pluck out his eyes, in a few years we we should have the nation full of blind beggars." When those in authority held such repressive opinions, it is no wonder that martyrdom soon followed in the track of Tyndale's New Testament —that it brought not peace, but a sword. In February 1528, at the very time Cuthbert Tonstal and his vicar-general were sitting in judgment upon the Word of God in London, it was also being condemned in Scotland by the martyrdom of Patrick Hamilton, the leader of the noble army of martyrs in the British Isles during the sixteenth century.

Patrick Hamilton, born in 1504, and the great-grandson of James the Second, received the elements of his education at St. Andrews, and afterwards studied on the Continent, chiefly at Paris and Louvaine. On his return to Scotland, to find his mother a widow, his father having been slain in the feud between the Douglases and the Hamiltons on the 30th April 1520, Patrick was again entered at St. Andrews, then the centre of ecclesiastical influence in Scotland, in whose castle the Primate resided, and there pursued his theological studies with special reference to the controversy regarding the doctrines of the Reformation, of which he had heard so much on the Continent. He was not at this early period inclined to Luther—he rather pre-
ferred

ferred Erasmus; but though he had been Abbot of Ferne from his boyhood, such was his hatred to monkish hypocrisy, that an old biographer says "he never assumed the monkish habit or resided with the monks." It is evident that Hamilton when he took orders had no thought of separating himself from the Romish Church, but it was not long before, like Luther, he was driven from her communion, as the conviction forced itself on him that allegiance to the Word of God and to the Pope were incompatible. With increased interest he continued his studies, and especially that of the Scriptures, though he had not as yet seen them in English. However, a copy of Tyndale's New Testament, one of those furtively brought into the country in bales of merchandise, at length fell into Hamilton's hands at St. Andrews, and rumours that he held heretical opinions soon reached Archbishop Beaton, who consequently caused "faithful inquisition" to be made, and discovered that Hamilton was infected with "heresy, disputing, holding, and manifesting divers heresies of Luther." His liberty and life being now in danger, Patrick Hamilton fled to Germany, and eventually reached Wittemberg, where he found himself side by side with Luther. The happy results which he now saw in Germany, as the fruit of the circulation of the

the Scriptures, both astonished and delighted him; the monasteries were deserted, and the churches, purified from Romish observances, now echoed with the voice of prayer and praise in a language which the people could understand.

From Wittemberg Hamilton went to Marburg, and became the friend of Francis Lambert, John Fryth, and of William Tyndale, the latter being then busy with his translation of the Old Testament. Hamilton's name stands among the earliest members of the University of Marburg, the first great school which, after the lapse of centuries, was established independently of Papal sanction. Late in the autumn of 1527, Hamilton returned to Scotland, with the resolve at any cost to expose the corruptions of Rome, and enforce "the reading of the Scriptures, and the necessity of repentance towards God and faith in Christ, in order to good works." The ardour with which Hamilton now preached the new doctrines, his learning, courtesy, blameless character, and noble birth, gave great weight to his teaching, and made him specially obnoxious to the clergy, who were panic-struck at his courage. These upholders of the "old learning" therefore determined to crush the heresy at once, lest it should take root in the land. Taking advantage of King James V.'s absence on a pilgrimage

age to St. Duthack's, Beaton summoned Hamilton from Ferne to St. Andrews, promising him safety; but Patrick's friends, seeing his danger, advised him to fly for his life. Not accepting this advice, Hamilton was arrested one night in bed, and carried to the Castle of St. Andrews. Next day, in the presence of the Cardinal, thirteen articles were laid to his charge by Alexander Campbell, a Dominican friar, an inveterate and mortal enemy of his; and during the examination the head and front of Hamilton's offending was proved to be, his having enforced the reading of the New Testament in English. On the same day on which his judges returned their verdict of guilty, Saturday, February 28, 1528, notwithstanding the Archbishop's promise, he was burnt at the stake, opposite St. Salvador's College, and his body reduced to ashes, before the sun went down.

The second martyr at St. Andrews, Henry Forrest, a Benedictine monk of Linlithgow, was also a young man. His martyrdom took place in 1533, "for nou uther crime but because he had ane New Testament in Engliss," and had been heard to say that Patrick Hamilton was a true martyr. "He suffered death at the north stile of the Abbey Church of St. Andrews, to the intent that all the people of Forfar and Angus might see the fire, and so might be the more feared from falling into the like doctrine, which they call heresy."

Throughout Scotland the martyrdom of Patrick Hamilton aroused much excitement, and nowhere was the feeling deeper than in St. Andrews itself, the Rome of Scotland, and it provoked inquiry everywhere into the reason why he had suffered, and in many cases inquiry led to the new doctrines being embraced. Among those who now cast in their lot with the "New Testamenters," as they began to be called, was Alexander Seaton, the king's confessor; and the clergy in consequence became generally more and more alarmed, wondering how it would all end. "My lord," said the shrewd John Lindsay to Archbishop Beaton, "if ye burn any more, except ye follow my counsel, ye will utterly destroy yourselves. If ye will burn them, let it be in how [hollow] cellars, for the reek [smoke] of Master Patrick Hamilton has infected as many as it blew upon." Despite this and similar warnings, an earnest search after heretics began, and for some years many of Scotland's nobility, as well as canons and friars, suffered martyrdom for the Protestant faith, while others recanted, fearing the terrible death which awaited them, and many more fled to England and to the Continent for shelter from their ecclesiastical persecutors.

During

During the years between 1529 and 1534, frequent traces are met with of the continued arrival of the New Testament. While searching for Tyndale at Cologne, copies of his translation were discovered, "which would," says the inquisitor, writing to Wolsey, "but for my interposition, have been pressed together, and covered over with flax, and, enclosed in packages, would, in time, without any suspicion, have been transmitted by sea into Scotland and England, and have been sold as merely waste paper." All through these years, the first decided controversy in Britain, which respected the right of every one, "both high and low, rich and poor together," to read the Scriptures in their own tongue, was being carried on. In the forefront of this controversy in Scotland was Alexander Ales, a priest and canon of the Cathedral of St. Andrews. He was but twenty-eight years old when the startling fact transpired that by means of prohibited books some canons and students were infected by the "new learning." Ales read the books to refute them, and when Patrick Hamilton was delivered unto death, he strove to reclaim him and save his life. But he failed; and, overcome by the arguments, and still more by the noble constancy of the martyr, he acknowledged himself conquered, and embraced the new doctrines. His faith was sorely tested,

tested, and after much endurance, he fled to Dundee, from which place he sailed for the Continent in 1531. Scarcely had Ales escaped, when the bishops issued an order to prohibit the New Testament from being read or sold in the country.

In England, as well as Scotland, the ecclesiastical authorities were at one on this matter—the repression of the Scriptures: and yet for some years past, in both countries, they had been welcomed, and held fast by multitudes even unto death; while, as if to show that the work was altogether independent of human control, those two men—William Tyndale, the English translator of the New Testament, and Alexander Ales, the principal advocate of its free circulation in Scotland, stood, as it were, aloof, both exiles in a strange land. Neither of them ever returned to their native countries, and Tyndale suffered martyrdom in 1536 at Vilvorde; but still the work went on.

The opposition in Scotland to the Bible continued to gather strength, and on the 8th June 1535, Parliament not only confirmed the Acts of 1525 and 1527 against prohibited books, but further enacted that "all persons having such books should deliver them up within forty days, under penalty of confiscation and imprisonment." "Discussion of opinions" was likewise forbidden, an exception being

being made in favour of "clerks in the schools," who might read in order to be able to refute them, and at length, in May 1536, the "reading of God's Word in the vulgar tongue was publicly prohibited." In spite of all this, many of the people were well-disposed to the Scriptures, and at midnight the "New Testamenters" assembled in secret—the Bible was brought from its hiding-place and read by one while the others listened around, and thus the Gospel took firm root throughout the land. Secular literature, in the form of popular songs and satirical verse, was also brought into the service of the Reforming party, and this contributed greatly to expose the ignorance, superstition, and immorality of the Romish clergy of the time.* These rhymes and ballads being easily committed to memory, were repeated from one to another—no small advantage to the cause at a time when the then young

---

* Ignorant, however, as the Scottish clergy were, they were perhaps not more so than many on the Continent at the same time. "A foreign monk, declaiming one day in the pulpit against Lutherans and Zuinglians, said to his audience: A new language was *invented some time ago*, which has been the mother of all these heresies—the Greek. A book is printed in this language, called the New Testament, which contains many dangerous things. *Another language is now forming*, the Hebrew; whoever learns it immediately becomes a Jew."—*M'Crie's Life of Knox.*

young art of printing was under ecclesiastical control.

In this way perhaps the writings of Sir David Lyndsay had probably the most influence upon the Scottish Reformation, as these were universally popular, and though the bishops managed to have several laws passed against the circulation of his rhymes, they long outlived their enemies. Lyndsay's longest and gravest work, "Ane Dialog betuix Experience and Ane Courteour," is in a lofty tone, and in this poem "Experience" reviews the history of all the mighty bygone kingdoms; there being also a strong appeal in favour of the translation of the Scriptures into the vernacular tongue, from which there follows an extract, slightly modernised in spelling:

> "Prudent Saint Paul doth make narration,
>   Touching the divers Leed of every land,
> Saying there have been more edification
>   In five words, that folk do understand,
>   Then to pronounce of words ten thousand
> In strange language, and knows not what it means;
> I think such prattling is not worth two preens.
>
> "Unlearned people on the holy day,
>   Solemnedly they hear the Evangell sung,
> Not knowing what the Priest doth sing or say,
>   But as a Bell when that they hear it rung;
>   Yet would the Priests in their mother tongue

Passe to the Pulpet, and that doctrine declare
To Laicke people, it were more necessare.

" I would that Prelates and Doctors of the Law
  With Laicke people were not discontent,
Though we into our vulgar tongue did knaw
  Of Christ Jesus the Lyfe and Testament,
  And how that we should keep commandement.
But in our language let us pray and read
Our Pater noster, Ave, and our Creed.

" I would some Prince of great discretion,
  In vulgar language plainly causde translate
The needful Lawes of this Region :
  Then would there not be halfe so great debate
  Among us people of the low estate.
If every man the verity did knawe,
We needed not to treat these men of Law.

" To do our neighbour wrong, we would beware,
  If we did fear the Lawes punishment :
There would not be such brawling at the Bar,
  Nor men of Law clime to such Royal rent,
  To keep the Law : if all men were content,
And each man do as he would be done to,
The Judges would get little thing adoe.

" The prophet David King of Israel,
  Compylde the pleasant Psalmes of the Psalter
In his own proper tongue, as I here tell :
  And Solomon, which was his Son and Haire,
  Did make his Book into his tongue vulgare :
Why should not their sayings be to us shown
In our language, I would the cause were known.

           " Let

> " Let Doctors write their curious questions,
>   And arguments sown full of sophistries,
> Their Logick, and their high opinions,
>   Their dark judgements of Astronomie,
>   Their Medicine, and their Philosophie ;
> Let Poets show their glorious engine,
> As ever they please, in Greek or in Latine.
>
> " But let us have the books necessare
>   To Common-wealth and our Salvation
> Justly translated in our tongue vulgare ;
>   And eke I make you supplication,
>   O gentle Reader, have none indignation,
> Thinking to meddle with so high matter.
> Now to my purpose forward will I fare."

Among the many efforts of the intolerant ecclesiastical party, reference may be here made to one which was put forth on the 2d March 1558, when a provincial Synod—worthy of notice as the last ever held in Scotland during Roman Catholic times—was held in the Black Friars' Church, to consult regarding measures for preserving the faith against the Reforming party of the " Congregation." Amongst other things decreed by this Synod, was the denouncing of Sir David Lyndsay's works, which were ordered to be burnt. No doubt the poet deserved some such reprisal at their hands, for he was very severe on the ignorant Romish clergy of his time, as in the satirical poem of " Kittie's

"Kittie's Confession," wherein an ignorant father-confessor is alluded to with sly humour :

> "He speirit monie strange case,
> How that my lufe did me embrace. . . .
> He me absolvit for ane plack,
> Thocht he with me na price wad mak ;
> And mekil Latine did he mummill ;
> I heard na thing but hummill bummill."

But the poet was already in his grave when his writings were thus condemned—Lyndsay having died, it is supposed, about the end of 1557. Previous to the Reformation, the corruptions of the Church had risen to a greater height in Scotland than in any other nation within the pale of the Western Church ; and the abuses in morals, together with differences in purely religious matters, had much to do with the spread of the Reforming doctrines. Yet there were other causes at work also, of a perhaps more practical nature. There was, first, the collision between the higher ecclesiastics and the nobility ; for a long time the latter had seen their property and their power taken from them to enrich the priesthood, and when a set of teachers arose who taught that the clergy had no right to the position and wealth they had assumed, the nobles were very willing to be convinced. As regards the poorer classes, again, the tithes and other

other dues exacted by the Church had long been felt to be a grievous burden, and they were thus

SIR DAVID LYNDSAY.*

also ready enough to follow in the track of their native nobility.

Besides

---

* From frontispiece to Pinkerton's "Scottish Poems." 3 vols. London, 1792.

Besides the poet Lyndsay, many persons of rank had thus adopted the new doctrines previous to 1540, among whom were the Earl of Glencairn, his son, Lord Kilmaurs, the Earl of Errol, Lord Ruthven, and others, several of whom narrowly escaped the fate of Patrick Hamilton. They probably would have suffered, had not King James V. himself died on the 14th December 1542. Upon the death of the king, Cardinal Beaton presented to the nobility a forged will, in the hope that by this means he might procure the regency of the kingdom for himself during the minority of the infant Queen Mary. His scheme failed, for within forty-eight hours after the burial of James V. on the 8th January, James Hamilton, the second Earl of Arran, was proclaimed Protector and Governor of the kingdom, and the defeated Cardinal was thrown into prison for a time. Shortly after, on the 12th March 1543, "the most substantious Parliament that ever was seen in Scotland in any man's remembrance" was called together. Business began on a Tuesday, and lasted only for three days. On the last day, Robert, Lord Maxwell, a nobleman well disposed towards the New Testamenters, though, while Beaton was in full sway, he was careful to avoid gaining notoriety regarding his opinions, brought in a bill to allow "the Scriptures

Scriptures to be read by all, without any limitation," and " in the vulgar tongue." This proposal met with fierce opposition from the ecclesiastics present in Parliament, but in spite of all their efforts the bill passed, and stands to this day unrepealed in the statute-book of the country. This bill was in part as follows:

"It is statute, and ordanit, that it sal be lefull to all our sovirane ladyis leiges to have the haly writ, to wit, the New Testament and the Auld, in the vulgar toung, in Inglis, and Scotis, of an gude and trew translation, and that thai sal incur na crimes for the hefing and reding of the samen; providing always that na man dispute, or hald opinizeonis under the pains conteinit in the actis of parliament. The lordis of Articklis beand avisit with the said writting, finds the samin resonable, and therefore thinkis that the samin may be usit amongis all the lieges of this realme of our vulgar toung, of an gude, trew, and just translation, because there was na law shewn, nor producit in the contrar; and that none of our soverane ladyis legiges incur ony crimes for haifing, or reding of the samin, in form as said is, nor sall be accusit therefor in time coming; and that na personis dispute, argou, or hold oppunionis of the samin, under the saidis painis containit in the foresaidis actis of parliament."

The Regent's proclamation, on the 19th March 1543, regarding this bill was as follows:

"*Clerk of Register.*—It is our will and we charge you, that

that ye gar proclaim this day in the mercat cross of Edinburgh, the Acts made in our Sovereign lady's Parliament, that should be proclaimed and given forth to her lieges; and in special, the Act made for having of the New Testament in vulgar tongue, with certain additions, and thereafter give forth the copies thereof authentic, as effeiris, to all them that will desire the samyn, and insert this our command and charge in the books of Parliament for your warrant. Subscrivit with our own hand at Edinburgh, the 19th day of March, the year of God 1543 years.

"JAMES G[UBERNATOR]."

Still there was in this Act a certain limitation, in so far that while liberty was granted to read the Scriptures, it forbade all discussion upon the doctrines taught in them, under the pains contained in the former Acts of Parliament, and this limitation proved to be a source of much trouble in after years. Looking back upon the passing of this bill of March 1543, some twenty-five years afterwards, John Knox writes of the memorable event: "This was no small victory of Christ Jesus, fighting against the enemies of His verity: not small comfort to such as were before holden in such bondage, that they durst not have read the Lord's Prayer, the ten commandments, nor the articles of their faith in the English tongue, but they should have been accused of heresy. Then might have been

been seen the Bible lying upon almost every gentleman's table; the New Testament was borne about in many men's hands."

On the 3rd September 1543, the Earl of Arran, at the Franciscan convent of Stirling, publicly renounced all connection and abjured all sympathy with the Reformed religion; and being now reconciled to Beaton, at the same time received absolution at the hands of the Primate, whom he had proclaimed a traitor and had thrown into prison in the preceding January. The Cardinal having regained authority, it is not surprising that persecution, more bitter and more relentless than hitherto, set in anew against those who dared to express opinions contrary to the dogmas of the Church of Rome. It was then that George Wishart, one of the boldest among the promoters of the Reformation, suffered martyrdom, March 28, 1546—hurried to death without even the semblance of a trial by Cardinal Beaton, who was himself in the May following assassinated at St. Andrews, and with his death the worst features of the evil tyranny of the Romish Church in Scotland came to an end.

It is not to be wondered at that during those dark days of persecution no edition of the entire Bible, or even of the New Testament separately,
was

was ever printed at the Scottish press, now many years in existence, though copies of these were to be found in almost every parish in Scotland. It was not till 1579—thirty-three years after the death of Beaton, its bitter enemy, and seven after the death of Knox, its friend and advocate, that the first copy of the Bible was printed in Scotland.

CHAPTER II.

Translations of the Bible.

ANY attempts were made during the Middle Ages to satisfy the constant desire of religious people to possess the Scriptures in their native tongue, and translations of the Bible in manuscript were made by Wickliffe, Nicolas de Hereford, and John Purvey. These again were copied by friendly hands, and distributed amongst eager purchasers throughout the country. Bitter opposition was made to the circulation of these MS. Bibles, which never indeed could be very plentiful—the labour of transcription being so great—and the possession of a copy involving risks so serious, it became even dangerous to possess them; but all the zeal which the opponents of the Scriptures could display was not sufficient to destroy every copy, or tread down the sparks of spiritual life which had been kindled by their perusal. Just at this time, when the European mind was waking up from the sleep of ages, and new ideas

eager

eager for dissemination could not wait the slow and uncertain quill of the copyist, and when the Book had been rendered into the native tongue, the needful instrument for its wide-spread diffusion was invented. At the fitting epoch in God's providence, the art of printing was discovered, and soon proved, with its speed of impression and power of multiplication, the best handmaid for the dissemination of the truth; among the first, if not the very first complete volume which the art gave to the world being a Latin Bible—now called by way of distinction the "Mazarin Bible"—whose date is about 1450. Within a few years after this, Bibles were printed in France, Italy, Holland, and Germany in the native languages; but these, valuable as they were to their own countries, were of less value than that which was afterwards given to England, being made generally from Latin MS. Bibles, and therefore faulty and imperfect; while the first one given to this country was translated directly from the original Hebrew and Greek. The Old Testament in Hebrew appeared in a complete form at Soncino in 1488, and various portions of the New Testament in Greek were now and again issued, such as that of the printer Aldus, who in 1504 issued the first six chapters of John's Gospel; but it was not till about seventy years after the discovery of the art of of printing by movable type that there appeared an entire copy of the New Testament in Greek. This was the edition of Erasmus, professor of Greek at Cambridge, who prepared it from a few MSS. which he had at his command, and he had it printed at Basle in 1516. The publication of this Greek Testament by Erasmus may be said to have begun a new epoch in the history of Western Christendom.

The time for England was come—the materials for a translation into English from the original languages direct were now within reach, and a man equal to the work and willing to undertake it was not long in appearing. William Tyndale, born in Gloucestershire, educated at Oxford, and a pupil of Erasmus at Cambridge, was so fully alive to the need of an English version of the Scriptures that the desire to supply it became the one ambition of his life. Tyndale's character was in harmony with his pursuits and intellectual abilities; "his manners and conversation were such that all who knew him respected and esteemed him to be a man of most virtuous disposition and life unspotted." He received little favour or encouragement in the work to which he purposed to devote himself from those whose aid and influence he sought. Cuthbert Tonstal, Bishop of London, to whom Tyndale re-
sorted

sorted about 1522, could afford no shelter for such a worker; and he soon discovered that there was no place in his native country where he might translate the sacred book. Forced into exile, Tyndale travelled to Hamburg early in 1524, where he resided some months, spending his time in the great work to which he had devoted his life; and he soon gave to the world his translation of Matthew's Gospel, then that of Mark, which shortly after reached England and produced a favourable impression. Late in the year 1524, Tyndale went to Cologne, and having completed his translation of the whole New Testament, it was there put into the hands of the printers. The type was set up, several of the sheets were printed off, when a threatened seizure compelled Tyndale to escape with his printed sheets and blocks to Worms, where the enthusiasm for Luther and the Reformation was then at its height, in which place no time was lost in furthering the work, and a large edition was soon ready for transport to England. In spite of a most vigilant watch along the coasts of Scotland and England, numerous copies of this translation found their way, in cases, in barrels, in bales of cloth, in sacks of flour, and every secret way that could be devised, into the country, and were scattered far and

The gospell of S. Mathew.
The fyrst Chapter.

Thys ys the boke of the generacion of Jesus Christ the sonne of David/ The sonne also of Abraham. ¶ Abraham begatt Isaac: Isaac begatt Jacob: Jacob begatt Judas and hys brethren: Judas begat Phares: and Zaram of thamar: Phares begatt Esrom: Esrom begatt Aram: Aram begatt Aminadab: Aminadab begatt naasson: Naasson begatt Salmon: Salmon begatt boos of rahab: Boos begatt obed of ruth: Obed begatt Jesse: Jesse begatt david the kynge: ¶ David the kynge begatt Solomon/ of her that was the wyfe of vry: Solomon begat roboam: Roboam begatt Abia: Abia begatt asa: Asa begatt iosaphat: Josaphat begatt Joram: Joram begatt Osias: Osias begatt Joatham: Joatham begatt Achas: Achas begatt Ezechias: Ezechias begatt Manasses: Manasses begatt Amon: Amon begatt Josias: Josias begatt Jechonias and his brethren about the tyme of the captivite of babilon ¶ After they were led captive to babilon / Jechonias begatt

Cha. ¶ Abraham and David are fyrst rehearsid/ because that christe was chefly promysed vnto them.

Saynct mathew leveth out certeyne generacions/ & describeth Christes linage from Solomon/ after the lawe of Moses/ but Lucas describeth it accordyng to nature/ fro nathan solomons brother. For the lawe calleth them a mannes childre which his broder begatt of his wyfe lefte behynde hym after his death. deu. xxv. c.

Facsimile of first page of Tyndale's Testament.

and wide, being sought after by men of all ranks and degrees.

Living in a city where there was a large Jewish population, Tyndale improved the opportunity by acquiring a mastery of the Hebrew language, and then proceeded to translate portions of the Old Testament. These show evident marks of care and patience, and the various notes and interpretations given with the text evidence signs of an acute, original, and painstaking scholarship. Tyndale's work was very different from Luther's —Luther being mighty by tongue and pen, for he was a man of war, unwearied in assault, and dealing out to opponents unmeasured scorn and vituperation; while Tyndale, on the other hand, lived a life of tranquil toil in his study, earnestly working on the one Book of divine truth, which he sent forth " to be known and read of all men." If he did not enter the lists of controversy an active champion like Luther, he wielded a still mightier power when he despatched across " the silver streak of sea " the English Bible, that the people might have and read the simple, plain, and profitable Word of Scripture.

Tyndale's English is decidedly superior to the writings of his time which have come down to us; his Bible is a noble translation, the basis of every subsequent

subsequent English version, and in several respects better than all succeeding versions. It has an individuality as pronounced as Luther's; its Saxon is racy and strong, sometimes majestic, and, above all, it is hearty and true; the reader feels that the translator felt what he wrote, that his heart was in his work, and that he strove to reproduce in his own mother-tongue what he believed to be the true sense of the Word of God as he understood it. "The peculiar genius," says Mr. Froude, "which breathes through the English Bible, the mingled tenderness and majesty, the Saxon simplicity, the grandeur, unequalled, unapproached in the attempted improvements of modern scholars—all are here, and bear the impress of the mind of one man, and that man William Tyndale."

A few specimens of Tyndale's verses are here given:

"And Mary sayde, My soule magnifieth the Lorde, and my sprete rejoyseth in God my Savioure.

For he hath loked on the povre degre off his honde mayden. Beholde now from hens forthe shall all generacions call me blessed.

For he that is myghty hath done to me greate thinges, and blessed ys his name:

And hys mercy is always on them that feare him thorow oute all generacions.

He hath shewed strengthe with his arme; he hath
          scattered

scattered them that are proude in the ymaginacion of their hertes.

He hath putt doune the myghty from their seates, and hath exalted them of low degre.

He hath filled the hongry with good thinges, and hath sent away the ryche empty.

He hath remembred mercy, and hath holpen his servaunt Israhel.

Even as he promised to oure fathers, Abraham and to his seed for ever."

"Oure Father which arte in heven, halowed be thy name. Let thy kingdom come. Thy wyll be fulfilled, as well in erthe, as hit ys in heven. Geve vs this daye oure dayly breade. And forgeve vs oure treaspases, even as we forgeve them which treaspas vs. Leede vs not into temptacion, but delyvre vs from yvell. Amen."

Revelation ii. 12–17.

"And to the messenger of the congregacion in Pergamos wryte: This sayth he whiche hathe the sharp swearde with two edges.

I knowe thy workes and where thow dwellest, evyn where Sathans seat ys, and thou kepest my name and hast not denyed my fayth. And in my dayes Antipas was a faythfull witnes of myne, which was slayne amonge you where sathan dwelleth.

But I have a fewe thynges agaynst the: that thou hast there, they that mayntayne the doctryne of Balam whiche taught in balake, to put occasion of syn before
the

the chylderne of Israhell, that they shulde eate of meate dedicat vnto ydoles, and to commyt fornicacion.

Even so hast thou them that mayntayne the doctryne of the Nicolaytans, whiche thynge I hate.

But be converted or elles I will come vnto the shortly and will fyght agaynste them with the swearde of my mouth.

Let him that hath eares heare what the sprete sayth vnto the congregacions: To him that ouercommeth will I geve to eate manna that is hyd, and will geve him a whyte stone, and in the stone a newe name wrytten, whych no man knoweth, saving he that receaveth it."

The introduction of Tyndale's translations assumed such proportions that the zeal of the clergy against them found vent in England, as it had in Scotland, in most violent and very unecclesiastical measures, which resulted not only in burning the books themselves, but also brought many of their readers to the flames. At the treaty of Cambray in 1529, where Bishop Tonstal and Hackett were among the representatives of England, it was stipulated that the contracting parties were not "to print or sell any Lutheran books on either side." Tonstal took Antwerp on his way to England, and to that visit is referred the following incident, narrated by Halle in his Chronicle. The Bishop sought out Augustus Pakington, a mercer and merchant

merchant trading between Antwerp and London, and asked him as to the best way of securing the English Testaments for the purpose of burning and destroying them. "My lord," said Pakington, who was a secret friend of Tyndale, "if it be your pleasure, I could do in this matter probably more than any merchant in England; so if it be your lordship's pleasure to pay for them— for I must disburse money for them—I will ensure you to have every book that remains unsold."

"Gentle Master Pakington," said the Bishop, 'deemyng that he hadde God by the toe, whanne in truthe he hadde, as after he thought, the devyl by the fiste,'* "do your diligence and get them for me, and I will gladly give you whatever they may cost; for the books are naughty, and I intend surely to destroy them all, and to burn them at Paul's Cross."

A week or two later Pakington sought the translator, whose funds he knew were low. "Master Tyndale," he said, "I have found you a good purchaser for your books."

"Who is he?" asked Tyndale.

"My lord of London."

"But

---

* Halle's Chronicle.

"But if the Bishop wants the books it must only be to burn them."

"Well," was the reply, "what of that? The Bishop will burn them anyhow, and it is best that you should have the money for the enabling you to imprint others instead."

And so the bargain was made. "The Bishop had the books, Pakington had the thanks, and Tyndale had the money." "I am the gladder," said Tyndale, "for these two benefits shall come thereof. I shall get money to bring myself out of debt, and the whole world will cry out against the burning of God's Word, and the overplus of the money that shall remain with me shall make me more studious to correct the said New Testament, and so newly to imprint the same once again, and I trust the second will be much better than ever was the first."

The old Chronicler goes on to tell that "after this Tyndale corrected the same Testaments again, and caused them to be newly imprinted, so that they came thick and threefold into England. The Bishop sent for Pakington again, and asked how the Testaments were still so abundant. 'My lord,' replied the merchant, 'it were best for your lordship to buy up the stamps too by the which they are imprinted.'"

Translations of the Bible.   51

It is with evident enjoyment that Halle presents us with another scene as a sequel to the story.

BURNING THE BIBLES AT PAUL'S CROSS.

A prisoner, a suspected heretic named Constantine, was

was being tried a few months later before Sir Thomas More. "Now, Constantine," said the judge, "I would have thee to be plain with me in one thing that I shall ask, and I promise thee I will show thee favour in all other things whereof thou art accused. There are beyond the sea Tyndale, Joye, and a great many of you; I know they cannot live without help. There must be some that help and succour them with money, and thou, being one of them, hadst thy part thereof, and therefore knoweth from whence it came. I pray thee, tell me who be they that help them thus?"

"My lord," quoth Constantine, "I will tell thee truly—it is the Bishop of London that hath holpen us, for he hath bestowed among us a great deal of money upon New Testaments to burn them, and that hath been our chief succour and support."

"Now, by my troth," said Sir Thomas More, "I think even the same, for I told the Bishop thus much before he went about it."

The opponents of the book began at last to see that a printed Testament continually being produced was quite beyond their power to destroy. Bishop Tonstal profited by his lesson, and instead of buying and burning the book any longer, he preached a famous sermon at Paul's Cross, declaring its "naughtiness," and asserting that he himself

himself had found in it more than two thousand errors;* and at the close of his sermon he hurled the copy which he held into a great fire that blazed before him.

Tyndale, after his residence at Worms, next went to the quaint old town of Marburg, in the valley of the Lahn, where he appears to have remained for about two years, working with his friend John Fryth at the Pentateuch, besides printing here also his "Practice of Prelates." After this he again returned to Hamburg, where various endeavours were made by the ecclesiastical authorities of England to induce Tyndale to return home on certain proposed conditions. These efforts failing, the aim henceforth was to get him arrested, and throughout all the turmoil and trouble to which he was at this time subjected, the brave old man still proceeded with his work of translation. In 1533 Tyndale was for a short time at Nürnberg for the sake of printing, and then again at Antwerp, where he was liberally provided for by the English merchants. Four editions of his New Testament were

---

* "There is not so much as one i therein," Tyndale said in reply to this attack, "if it lack the tittle over its head, but they have noted and number it to the ignorant people for a heresy."

were printed at Antwerp in 1534. At last the long search and crafty intrigues of his enemies succeeded, and Tyndale was treacherously seized at the house of his friend Poyntz at Antwerp towards the autumn of 1535, and sent to the castle of Vilvorde. In October 1536 Tyndale was condemned, strangled, and burnt—his last words being the prayer, " Lord, open the King of England's eyes."

> " Patriots have toiled, and in their country's cause
> Bled nobly, and their deeds, as they deserve,
> Receive proud recompense. We give in charge
> Their names to the sweet lyre. . . .
> But martyrs struggle for a brighter prize,
> And win it with more pain. Their blood is shed
> In confirmation of the noblest claim,—
> Our claim to feed upon immortal truth,
> To walk with God, to be divinely free,
> To soar, and to anticipate the skies.
> Yet few remember them. They lived unknown
> Till Persecution dragged them into fame,
> And chased them up to heaven. Their ashes flew
> —No marble tells us whither. With their names
> No bard embalms and sanctifies his song ;
> And history, so warm on meaner themes,
> Is cold on this. She execrates indeed
> The tyranny that doomed them to the fire,
> But gives the glorious sufferers little praise." *

No

---

* Cowper's " Task."

No grander life than Tyndale's shows itself in the whole annals of the Reformation—none which comes nearer in its beautiful self-forgetfulness to His who "laid down His life for His sheep," and no higher honour could be given to any man than the accomplishment of such a work as that to which he gave himself. All the earlier English translations were but translations of a translation, and Tyndale was the first to go back to the original Hebrew and Greek, though the MSS. accessible to him were not of so much authority or value as those available in these latter days. Every succeeding version is in reality little more than a revision of Tyndale's, and his New Testament was a noble aid to the early advancement of the cause of the Reformation in Scotland, and greatly influenced the passing of the Act allowing a free Bible in that country.

Another most important translation of the Bible made its appearance in October 1535, bearing the name of Miles Coverdale. This was the very first entire Bible which had been seen in print, and is on this account remarkable. Tyndale's New Testament, with several of the books of the Old Testament, were to be had by this time, but Miles Coverdale gave to the people for the first time in one volume the Word of God complete in their own tongue.

It is not known where this Bible was first printed, but it is very generally supposed to have been done in some foreign city, and some have asserted that it was printed by Christian Egenolph at Frankfort. Coverdale makes no pretence that his Bible is an original translation, and does not conceal that "it is translated out of Douche* and Latin into English," with the help of "five sundry interpreters" (translators); the chief of these interpreters being evidently William Tyndale, whom, in the New Testament, Coverdale closely follows.

Although Coverdale's version was thus only secondary, it possessed merits of its own; and not a little of that indefinable quality that gives popular charm to our English Bible, and has endeared it to so many generations, is owing to Coverdale. The characteristic features are Tyndale's in all their boldness of form and expression, the more delicate lines and shadings are the contribution of Coverdale, both in his own version, and in the Great Bible which he afterwards revised and edited. The version of Coverdale is also known as the "Treacle Bible," from the rendering of the twenty-second verse of Jeremiah viii.:

"Is

---

* *Douche* at that time meant what is now called German, not Low German or Dutch.

"Is there no triacle in Galaad?" A few other passages which appear quaint to modern readers may also be quoted: "And she bare it [an olive leaf] in her nebb," Gen. viii. 11; "Cast a pece of a mylstone upon Abimelech's heade and brake his brain panne," Judges ix. 53; "And stackered towarde the dores of the gate, and his slaveringes ranne downe his beerde," 1 Sam. xxi. 13; "The foolish bodyes saye in their hertes, Tush, there is no God," Psalm xiv. 1; "Thou shalt not nede to be afrayde of ony bugges by night," Psalm xci. 5; "So that they shal breake their swerdes and speares, to make sythes, sycles, and sawes thereof," Isaiah ii. 4; "The erth shal geue a greate crack, it shal haue a sore ruyne, and take an horrible fall," Isaiah xxiv. 20; "Because their wyddowes were not looked vpon in the daylie hand-reachinge," Acts vi. 1; "But waysteth his brayne aboute questions and stryuynges of wordes," 1 Tim. vi. 4, &c.

The time of Coverdale was one of great progress in every respect; but in no one branch of knowledge was there a more perceptible advance than in that of Biblical learning. Following upon Coverdale's, "Matthews' Bible" appeared in 1537. This Bible was really prepared by John Rogers, one of the early Reformers, who afterwards was the first person condemned as a heretic in the reign of Queen

Queen Mary, and was burnt at Smithfield, February 1, 1555. "Matthews'" work was Tyndale's translation pure and simple, all but part of the Old Testament, which, with some alteration, is taken from Coverdale. Shortly after appeared "Taverner's Bible," which was little more than an edition of Matthews', with its notes either omitted or toned down.

None of these versions were satisfactory, and so it came about that Cranmer and some of Henry VIII.'s chief advisers set their hearts upon a translation worthy of the position of a National Bible. Miles Coverdale was selected to take charge of this one, which became known as the "Great Bible," or "Cranmer's Bible," and he went to Paris with the King's printer, that the book might be produced in the best style of the time. The Inquisitor-General, however, got notice of the project, and the result was that Coverdale carried off the printing-press, types, and the printers themselves to complete the work in England. It may be described as a compilation from Matthews' and Coverdale's Bibles, or as a revision of Matthews' by Coverdale, and hence, as Matthews' was almost entirely Tyndale's version, the Great Bible after all was really little more than a revised edition of Tyndale!

"Thus

Translations of the Bible.

"Thus had the old martyr triumphed. Only a few years had elapsed since he had been brought to his death, and here was his Bible, authorised by the King, commended by the clergy, and placed in the parish churches for the teaching of the people! And as if to mark the change with all the emphasis that was possible, an inscription on the title told that 'it was oversene and perused at the commandement of the King's Highness by the ryghte reverende fathers in God, Cuthbert bishop of Duresme (Durham), and Nicholas bishop of Rochester.'" And this Bishop Cuthbert was none other than Cuthbert Tonstal, Tyndale's untiring opponent and persecutor, who had bargained with Pakington to purchase the New Testaments, and had hurled into the flames from the pulpit at Paul's Cross the translation which now went forth with royal approval to the people.

The desire to read or listen to the words of Holy Writ in their own tongue had now become so intense, that crowds would often gather round one who was able to read the large Bible set up, and frequently chained, to a pillar in the churches. Even Bishop Bonner was so moved by the popular wish as "to set up in certain convenient places in St. Paul's Church six large Bibles," so that the people might come there and learn for themselves

themselves their duties and privileges as Christians.

This halcyon period was not of long duration, and shortly after the publication of the Great Bible a reaction set in, when all translations bearing the name of Tyndale were proscribed,—a prohibition which King Henry VIII. renewed in 1546, and at this time included Coverdale's New Testament along with the books of Tyndale. The Great Bible thus alone remained unforbidden, though severe restrictions were laid upon its use, and it is believed that this was the cause of a great destruction of the earlier Bibles and Testaments, while even where the books have been preserved, in a number of cases the titles have been taken out, so that the true character of the volume might escape the observation of a hasty and ignorant inquisitor.*

King Henry VIII. died in January 1547, and was succeeded by Edward VI., in whose short reign of six and a half years the restrictions were greatly removed, and many editions of the Bible were printed,

---

* A copy of Miles Coverdale's Bible, issued in 1535, was sold recently in London for £120. No perfect copy of this Bible is known to exist, and the one sold on this occasion had the title, first few leaves, and map in facsimile.

THE CHAINED BIBLE.

printed, but no new translation was undertaken. Then followed the dark period of Queen Mary, when no Bible was permitted to be printed, and by various proclamations the public or open reading of the Scriptures was prohibited, and when those who had been earnestly striving to put God's Word into the hands of the people had to yield up their lives at the stake, or flee from their native land to foreign countries. How Queen Mary and her minions dealt with the Bible may be learned from the following edict issued by Bishop Bonner in October 1554: "Because some children of iniquity, given up to carnal desires and novelties, have by many ways enterprised to banish the ancient manner and order of the Church, and to bring in and establish sects and heresies; taking from thence the picture of Christ, and many things besides instituted and observed of ancient time laudably in the same; placing in the room thereof such things, as in such a place it behoved them not to do; and also have procured, as a stay to their heresies (as they thought), certain Scriptures wrongly applied to be painted upon the church walls; all which persons tend chiefly to this end—that they might uphold the liberty of the flesh, and marriage of priests, and destroy, as much as lay in them, the reverent sacrament of the altar, and might extinguish and
enervate

enervate holy-days, fasting-days, and laudable discipline of the Catholic Church; opening a window to all vices, and utterly closing up the way unto virtue: wherefore we, being moved with a Christian zeal, judging that the premises are not to be longer suffered, do, for discharge of our duty, commit unto you jointly and severally, and by the tenor hereof do straitly charge and command you, that at the receipt hereof, with all speed convenient, you do warn, or cause to be warned, first, second, and third time, and peremptorily, all and singular churchwardens and parishioners whosoever, within our aforesaid diocese of London (wheresoever any such Scriptures or paintings have been attempted), that they abolish and extinguish such manner of Scriptures, so that by no means they be either read or seen; and therein to proceed, moreover, as they shall see good and laudable in this behalf. And if, after the said monition, the said churchwardens and parishioners shall be found remiss and negligent, or culpable, then you, jointly and severally, shall see the foresaid Scriptures to be razed, abolished, and extinguished forthwith." This mandate was directed, of course, against the usage introduced in Edward VI.'s reign, of writing Scripture texts on the walls of the churches; and as a favourite inscription was one which bore especially against Romish

Translations of the Bible.

Romish superstition, 1 John v. 21, in Tyndale's version, "Babes, kepe youre selues from ymages," this may account for Bonner's severity.

Among those forced into exile through the terror of fire and sword were Coverdale and several others, who found a temporary home at Geneva; and these earnest men, free in this city to pursue their labours in comparative peace, and allowed to worship God according to their own convictions, set diligently to work in producing another English translation which should avoid the blemishes of either Tyndale's or the Great Bible. Both by day and by night, these learned and pious men engaged themselves with the arduous task—comparing former translations with the original tongues, and searching through the Hebrew and Greek MSS. then at Geneva, in order to detect any errors which might accidentally have been allowed to creep in. They were so diligent in their work that copies of the New Testament found their way into England, surreptitiously no doubt, before the death of Queen Mary, as appears from a declaration by John Living, a priest, who had been robbed in Paternoster Row of his purse, girdle, psalter, and a "New Testament of Geneva."

The labours of the exiled Reformers eventually produced a more complete and satisfactory translation of the Bible in 1560, with many important additions

additions and improvements, the New Testament portion being issued first in 1557. The chief burden of its expense was borne by the English congregation at Geneva, of which John Bodley, father of Sir Thomas Bodley, the founder of the Bodleian Library at Oxford, was a member who contributed generously; and he received a grant, on his return to England, of a patent for printing that edition for seven years. There was in this Bible a Dedication to Queen Elizabeth, quite free from the fulsome flattery which is so conspicuous in the one to King James, which afterwards appeared in the Authorised Version of 1611. There is also an "Address to the Christian Reader," describing the nature and features of the work, of which the following is part: "Yet lest either the simple should be discouraged, or the malicious haue any occasion of iust cauillation, seeing some translations reade after one sort, and some after another, whereby all may serue to good purpose and edification, we haue in the margent noted that diuersitie of speech or reading which may also seeme agreeable to the minde of the Holy Ghost, & proper for our language with this marke ‖. Againe, whereas the Ebrewe speeche seemed hardly to agree with ours, we haue noted it in the margent after this sort ‡, vsing that which was more intelligible. And albeit that

that many of the Ebrewe names be altered from the old text, & restored to the true writing & first originall, whereof they haue their signification yet in the vsuall names, little is changed for feare of troubling simple readers. Moreouer, whereas the necessitie of the sentence required any thing to be added (for such is the grace and proprietie of the Ebrewe & Greeke tongues that it cannot but either by circumlocution or by adding the verbe or some worde, be vnderstood of them that are not well practised therein), we haue put it in the text with another kinde of letter, that it may easily bee discerned from the common letter. As touching the diuision of the verses, we haue folowed the Ebrewe examples, which haue so euen from the beginning distinguished them. Which thing as it is most profitable for memorie, so doth it agree with the best translations, & is most easie to finde out both by the best Concordances, & also by the quotations which we haue diligently herein perused & set forth by this *. Besides this, the principall matters are noted and distinguished by this marke ¶. We haue also indeauoured both by the diligent reading of the best commentaries, & also by the conference with the godly & learned brethren, to gather briefe annotations vpon all the hard places, as well for the vnderstanding of such

words

words as are obscure, & for the declaration of the text, as for the application of the same, as may most appertaine to God's glorie, & the edification of his Church," &c.

This work, which commonly went under the name of the "Geneva Bible," was well received by all classes and soon gained a high reputation, and from the time of its first appearance became the household Bible of the English-speaking people, continuing to be so for nearly three-quarters of a century. Its size was more handy, and its cost more moderate, than the Great Bible, which thus soon lost its hold on the popular favour. Many editions of the Geneva version were published between 1560 and 1611, the date of King James's Authorised Version, and to the second edition of the Geneva in 1561 it is that we are indebted for the Bassandyne Bible, that which was first printed in Scotland.

CHAPTER III.

Introduction of Printing into Edinburgh.

IBERTY having at last been given by the Scottish Parliament, in March 1543, to the people to use the Bible in their own tongue, and a suitable complete version being now ready, it remains to be seen how this was accomplished, with the help of the new art of printing. Under the energetic government of James IV., Scotland for some years enjoyed the utmost tranquillity and prosperity. The King's amiable and popular manners, his enactment of wise and salutary laws, combined with his stern repression of the disorder and spoliation practised by the turbulent nobility, all contributed to render the reign of this gallant monarch one of the most auspicious the people of Scotland had ever experienced. Learning was looked upon with the highest favour by the Court, and literature was rapidly extending its influence under the zealous co-operation of Dunbar, Douglas, Lyndsay, Kennedy, and others.

others. The husbandman tilled his lands, and the merchant traversed the country with his goods in security, while the foreign trader visited the markets of the different burghs fearless of plunder or interruption. It was during this brief interregnum of freedom from the foreign and internecine strife which had always more or less been the general characteristic of Scottish history, that the invention of printing—that art which, perhaps more than any other human discovery, has changed the condition and destinies of the world—found its way into Scotland. James IV. evidently took an enthusiastic interest in every new invention, and it is known that he had a strong love for learning, being himself no mean scholar. In connection with this is found the earliest record of Androw Myllar, one of the first Scottish printers, which bears that on the 29th March 1503 he was paid the sum of ten pounds for certain Latin books supplied to the King; and at another time we find the King's treasurer ordered to pay fifty shillings "for iij. prentit bukis tane fra Andro Myllaris wyf." Interested thus in literature, King James could not look upon the new art with indifference, and it may have been brought more especially under his notice by Walter Chepman, seemingly a man of wealth and consequence, and evidently an officer

of

of the King's household, as his name frequently appears in the Accounts and Register of the Privy Seal after the year 1494.

The facts regarding the introduction of printing into Scotland were ascertained beyond dispute by the discovery, towards the end of last century, among the records in the Register House at Edinburgh, of the following patent, dated 15th September 1507, granted by James IV. to Walter Chepman and Androw Myllar, burgesses of Edinburgh:

"James, etc.—To al and sindrj our officiaris liegis and subdittis quham it efferis, quhais knawlage thir our lettres salcum, greting; Wit ye that forsamekill as our lovittis servitouris Walter chepman and Andro myllar burgessis of our burgh of Edinburgh, has at our instance and request, for our plesour, the honour and profitt of our Realme and liegis, takin on thame to furnis and bring hame ane prent, with all stuff belangand tharto, and expert men to use the samyne, for imprenting within our Realme of the bukis of our Lawis, actis of parliament, croniclis, mess bukis, and portuus efter the use of our Realme, with addicions and legendis of Scottis sanctis, now gaderit to be ekit tharto, and al utheris bukis that salbe sene necessar, and to sel the sammyn for competent pricis, be our avis and discretioun thair labouris and expens being considerit; And becaus we understand that this cannot be perfurnist without rycht greit cost labour and expens, we have grantit and promittit

to

to thame that thai sall nocht be hurt nor preventit tharon be ony utheris to tak copyis of ony bukis furtht of our Realme, to gir imprent the samyne in utheris cuntreis, to be brocht and sauld agane within our Realme, to cause the said Walter and Androu tyne thair gret labour and expens; And alis It is divisit and thocht expedient be us and our counsall, that in tyme cuming mess bukis, manualis, matyne bukis, and portuus bukis, efter our awin scottis use, and with legendis of Scottis sanctis, as is now gaderit and ekit by ane Reverend fader in god, and our traist consalour Williame bischope of abirdene and utheris, be usit generaly within al our Realme alssone as the sammyn may be imprentit and providit, and that na maner of sic bukis of Salusbery use be brocht to be sauld within our Realme in tym coming; And gif ony dois in the contrar, that thai sal tyne the sammyne; Quharfor we charge straitlie and commandis yow al and sindrj our officiaris, liegis, and subdittis, that nane of yow tak apon hand to do onything incontrar this our promitt, devise, and ordinance, in tyme cuming, under the pane of escheting of the bukis, and punising of thair persons bringaris tharof within our Realme, in contrar this our statut, with al vigour as efferis. Geven under our prive Sel at Edinburgh, the xv day of September, and of our Regne the xx^{ti} yer."—*Books of the Privy Seal*, iii. 129.

Only a short period after this, Scotland was at the mercy of her southern rival: her King was slain, the chief of her nobles and warriors had perished

perished at Flodden, on the 8th September 1513, and adversity and ignorance again replaced all the advantages which had followed the rule of James IV.

To what extent Chepman and Myllar made use of their patent cannot now be determined, but it is surmised that a number of works issued from their press; of these only two, however, were for a long time known—the earliest, a volume of metrical tales and ballads, such as were popular in those days, and of which the first tale in order is "The Porteous of Noblenes;" the other work being the "Breviarium Aberdonense." This Breviary consists of two volumes, and the first page begins—"*In nomine sanctæ et individuæ Trinitatis, Patris, et Filii, et Spiritus Sancti.* Breviarium ad usum et consuetudinem percelebris ecclesiæ cathedralis Aberdon. in Scotia, regnante principe nostro serenissimo Jacobo, quarto, divina favente clementia Scotorum rege illustrissimi, imperii sui anno vicesimo secundo, pro hyemali parte feliciter sumit exordium." At the end are these words: " Opido Edinburgensi impresso jussu et impensis honorabilis viri *Walteri Chepman* ejusdem opidi Mercatoris, quarto die mensis Junii, anno Domino millesimo ccccc decimo." There is on the back of this latter page an engraving of Chepman's device, representing

ing a savage man and woman at full length—their shoulders bare, their lower limbs clothed with skins of beasts, in their hands flower-stalks, and their heads wreathed with flowers. They are standing one on each side of a tree, from which hangs a shield with the cipher of W. C. At the bottom, between two black lines, are the words: "✠ *Walterus* ✠ *chepman* ℥." This kind of device was peculiar to French printers, and the cut agrees with those on several old French books, excepting the cipher. The italic words in the extracts above are printed with red ink in the original.

Of the four copies of the Breviary known to exist, all are defective, and it would barely be possible to form a complete copy out of the whole four; the only one possessing a title is that in the University Library at Edinburgh, and this only to the first volume.* It was not till 1788 that any earlier production of Chepman and Myllar's press than the Breviary was known, but in that year there

---

* "The 'Breviarium Aberdonense' seems to have established in Scotland something like the supremacy of the 'Usum Sarum' in England. The whole Breviary was reprinted in London in 1854, in two volumes quarto, making one of the finest specimens of facsimile-reprinting then in existence."—*Hill Burton.*

there was presented to the Advocates' Library the volume of ballads already referred to. There are in this book eleven separately printed small quartos, some of which indicate the printers and date of printing. The earliest dated piece, and the most complete one in the collection, has the following colophon :

> "Hier endis the maying and disport of chaucer. Emprentit in the southgait of Edinburgh be Walter chepman and Androw myllar the fourth day of aprile the yhere of god M.CCCCC. and viii. yheris."

Another, in six leaves quarto, bears the following title :

> "Hier begynnys ane litil tretie intitulit the goldyn targe compilit be Maister Wilyam dunbar."

These Ballads are printed from a Pica Black, in pages about the size of demy 8vo, and nothing can surpass the regularity of the letters, which are at once carefully formed and beautifully cast. The tracts, it is true, abound in errata, arising no doubt from the circumstance that they were composed, as well as read for press, by foreign workmen, but the press-work would put to shame many modern examples. Especially is this latter point true of
the

the Aberdeen Breviary, which is in a Longprimer Black type, in double columns, many of the pages having lines and paragraphs in red and black alternately. The Metrical Romances were reprinted, under the supervision of Dr. Laing, by Messrs. Ballantyne & Company in 1827; but after the volume was completed, a disastrous fire occurred in the binder's premises, which destroyed the greater portion of the sheets, so that only seventy-six copies (four of which are on vellum) were actually published, and of these not a few bore marks of the conflagration from which they had escaped. The volume, as reprinted, takes its name from the poem first in order—"The Knightly Tale of Golagros and Gawane;" and the following is a list of the contents:

- The Knightly Tale of Golagros and Gawane.
- The Goldyn Targe.
- The Flyting of Dunbar and Kennedy.
- The Twa Mariit Wlemen and the Wedo.
- The Ballad of Lord Barnard Stewart.
- The Traitie of Orpheus King.
- Ane Buke of Gud Counsale.
- The Maying, or Disport of Chaucer.
- Sir Eglamour of Arteas.
- A Gest of Robyn Hode.
- The Porteous of Noblenes.

The

The two works above-named, the Breviary and the Ballads, were long thought to have been the earliest in which Myllar had been engaged as the printer; but at Paris in 1869 a book entitled

DEVICE OF ANDROW MYLLAR.

"Expositio Sequentiarum" (dated 1506) was exposed for sale, which, though not indicating where or by whom it was printed, contains the name of Androw Myllar on the sill of the device, while the types are identical

identical with those used by Laurence Hostingue of Rouen, and also afterwards by Myllar. The book was bought for the British Museum for £40. Again, in 1878, there was found in a private library at Dinant, in Bretagne, a black-letter quarto of 62 folios, the Latin title of which means, "The Interpretation of many ambiguous words, by Master John of Garland, indispensably needful to the Grammarian and lover of Latin," &c., and having the colophon and device of "Androw Myllar of Scotland," "in the year of the Christian Redemption, One Thousand Five Hundred and Five." Evidently this also was printed at Rouen. These discoveries have led to the conjecture that at the time when King James bought the books from "Myllaris wyf," Androw himself was abroad gaining instruction in the art, and that, as Chepman was wealthy, he may have sent Myllar to Rouen, and on his return with presses and type, retained him as working partner in the printing-house they set up. The workshop of these two first printers was in the *south-gait* of Edinburgh, as appears from the colophon given on page 75; but whether the south-gait refers to the Cowgate or to the lower part of High Street is a controverted point. Dr. Robert Chambers states that the workshop of the first Scottish printers was in the Cowgate, near to where George IV. Bridge now

is,

is, and where not a few printing-offices in later times were established; while Dr. Laing is of opinion that their office was in High Street, near the head of Blackfriars' Wynd, and supports his view by a quotation from a license in the Registers of the Privy Seal to Chepman giving him power to have "stairis towart the Hie Strete and Calsay, with bak staris and turngres in the Frer Wynd, or on the forgait, of sic breid and lenth as he sall think expedient for entre and asiamentis to his land and tenement," &c. But as Chepman was wealthy, and possessed of considerable property, this license may have referred to alterations on another building than that in which the printing-house was situated; and as the south-gait is thought to have been only another name for Cowgate, the probability is in favour of the latter locality. Wherever their place of business was, however, we may suppose that visits were frequently paid to it by the gallant King James, where he saw types set, the ink-balls applied, proofs pulled, and chatted with the printers, and showed his delight at the new and astonishing art which was destined to work such wonders.

It affords conclusive evidence of the wealth of Chepman, and of the success which attended the art immediately after its introduction, that on the 21st of August 1513, Walter Chepman founded a chaplainry,

chaplainry, "for the welfare of the souls of the king, queen, and their offspring," at the altar of St. John the Evangelist, in an aisle built by him on the southern side of St. Giles' Church. Chepman also endowed another chaplainry to the memory of his royal master, James IV., in a Mortuary Chapel of the Holy Cross in the cemetery of St. Giles, in August 1528, the original deed of which is preserved in the city archives.

Some of Dunbar's poems were among the earliest productions that issued from the press of Chepman and Myllar, forming now very scarce and highly valued reliques of the art; and in his "Remonstrance to the King" there occurs an inventory which affords an insight into the crafts of Edinburgh in the time of James IV. A brief extract will suffice:

> " Cunyouris, carvouris, and carpentaris,
> Beildaris of barkis, and ballingaris;
> Masounis, lyand upon the land,
> And schip wrichtis hewand upone the strande;
> Glasing wrichtis, goldsmythis, and lapidaris,
> *Pryntouris*, payntouris, and potingaris," &c.

The introduction of printers into the above lines shows that the art was well known; and yet, for about thirty years after the Breviary, there is no actual evidence of the printing of books in Scotland, though

though the production of books in MS. seems to have been actively pursued; and, in fact, we find that the works of several Scottish writers were during this period printed on the Continent. It is difficult to account for this seeming discontinuance of printing after Chepman, who died in 1532 or 1533; probably the political distractions of the time may have contributed to render it unprofitable; but in its revival by Davidson in 1536 there was no deterioration, either in the importance of the works attempted, or in the manner in which the mechanical part was executed. There is perhaps but one exception to this complete cessation, in a book printed in Edinburgh about this time by John Story, called "The Office of Our Lady of Pity." It has been conjectured that Story was in the employment of Chepman, and succeeded to the business, since the type, as well as the arrangement and general appearance of Story's work, corresponds very much with the appearance of the Aberdeen Breviary; and it is probable other books were done which are now lost.

When Thomas Davidson, the next Scottish printer, appeared in 1536, one of his first works seems to have been a *Strena*, or Latin poem, written on the occasion of James V.'s accession. The only known copy of this book is in the British

British Museum. From the appearance of several of Davidson's books, it might seem, from the type he used being similar in size and character to that used by Chepman, that he had fallen heir to Chepman's "plant," more particularly as there is a look about the type which tells of having seen previous service; but closer scrutiny shows that while both used Black letter, Davidson's is slightly larger and of more modern design than that of Chepman. About 1540, the Scottish Parliament passed an Act ordaining the Lord Register to publish the Acts of Parliament passed in the reign of James V., and to employ what printer he pleased, providing the printer had the King's special license therefor—this Act being the last passed by King James V. The following is the special license granted to Davidson for this purpose:

"The copy of the Kingis grace licence and priuilege grantit to Thomas Dauidson, prentar, for imprenting of his gracis actis of parliament.

"JAMES be the grace of God King of Scottis, to all and sindry, quhom it efferis. Forsamekill as it is ordanit be ws, be an act maid in plane parliament, that all our actis maid be ws be publist outthrow al our realme; and that nane our shereiffis, stewardis, ballies, prouest, and baillies of oure burrowis, suld pretend ignorance throw misknawing thairof, that our clerk of registre, and counsel, suld

suld mak ane autentik copie of all sik actis as concernis the commoun weill of oure realme, and extract the samin under his subscription manuale, to be imprentit be quhat prentar it sall pleis him to cheis; prouiding alwayis, that the said prentar sall have oure speciall licence thairto, as in the said act at mair length is contenit.

"¶ We heirfore hes gevyn, and grantit, & be the tenour heirof gevis and grantis oure licence, to oure louit Thomas Dauidson, imprentar in oure burgh of Edinburgh, to imprent oure saidis actis of parliament, and dischargis all vther imprintaris, and writtaris, within yis oure realme, or without, present, and for to cum, to imprent, or writ our saidis actis of parliament, or bring thaym hame to be sauld, for the space of sex zeris next to cum, eftir the dait of thir presentis, under the pain of confiscatioun of the samyn. Subscrivit with oure hand, and gevin under oure priue seill, at Edinburgh, the sext day of December, and of oure regne the xxix zeir.

"¶ GOD KEIP THE KING."

The title of this work was: "The new actis and constitutionis of parliament, maid be the rycht excelent prince, James the fyft King of Scottis, 1540." On the same page are the Scots arms, above the crest the words "IN DEFENS," while on one side of the arms is "Jacobus," on the other "Rex 5." On the back of the title is the above license. At the end of the book is an engraving of Christ on the cross, surrounded by a number

of

of figures. The work contains the Acts of two Parliaments, "the former begunnyn and haldin at Edinburgh the vii day of Junii, the zeir of God MD and xxxv zeiris; the latter begunnyn and haldin at Edinburgh, the third day of December, the zeir of God MD and xl zeiris." The colophon bears "Imprentit in Edinburgh be Thomas Dauidson, dwellyng aboue the Nether Bow, on the North side of the gait, the aucht of Februarii, the zeir of God, 1541 zeiris." *

Davidson also printed between December 1541 and December 1542—though a former edition is said by Ames to have been done by him in 1536—Bellenden's translation of "The history and croniklis of Scotland, with the cosmography and dyscription thairof. Compilit be the nobill clerk, maister Hector Boece, channon of Aberdene. Translatit laitlie in our vulgar and commoun langage be maister Johne Bellenden, archedene of Murray, and channon of Ross; at the command of the richt hie, richt excellent, and nobill prince James the 5th of that name, king of Scottis; and imprentit in Edinburgh be me

---

* At the Woodhull Library sale, a thin folio of Scotch Acts of Parliament, printed in Black letter on vellum about the middle of the sixteenth century, was sold for 151 guineas.

me Thomas Dauidson, prentar to the Kingis nobyll grace, dwellyng fornens the Frere wynd [opposite the Blackfriars Wynd]. *Cum priuilegio.*"

Johne Skot, or Scott, was chronologically the next printer. He is believed by some to have been an Englishman, while other writers unhesitatingly pronounce in favour of his being a Scotchman, and a totally different person from a printer of the same name in London so early as 1521, and till 1537. The very year after the date of the London Scott's last book, 1538, there was printed at John Byddell's office, "at the signe of the Sonne, in Flete strete," "The Complaynte and Testament of a Popinjay," &c., a poem by Sir David Lyndsay —a circumstance which shows that there was some connection between Scotland and Byddell's establishment. Scott may have been engaged here, and have learned that there was then only one printer in Edinburgh, and consequently a favourable opening for starting a second press in that city. Whether he came to Edinburgh of his own accord, or by invitation, is uncertain, but it is the fact that in the following year, one Johannes Scot, designated impressor, received from the King a grant of two chambers, with cellars below, at the foot of Borthwick's Close, Cowgate.

Scott's stay in Edinburgh at this time does not appear

appear to have been of long duration, for in 1549 he printed at St. Andrews, under the eye of its reputed author, James Wedderburn, that remarkable little book, "The Complaynte of Scotland." In this work the author represents himself as wearied with study, and, to solace himself, "walking out into the wholesome fields to hear the songs of the shepherds." He then gives specimens of the songs of the period, a large number of which are now only known by name. From one of these early songs, called "Lustie Maye," a couple of verses are here given as an example of the verse of the time:

> "O, Lustie Maye, with Flora queen,
>   Whose balmy drops from Phœbus sheen
>   Prelusant beam before the day,
>   Before the day, the day;
>   By thee, Diana groweth green,
>   Through glaidness of this Lustie Maye,
>   Through glaidness of this Lustie Maye.
>
>   .   .   .   .   .
>
> "Of every monith in the year,
>   To mirthful Maye there is no peer,
>   Her glistening garments are so gay;
>   Garments so gay, so gay;
>   You lovers all make merrie cheer,
>   Through glaidness of this Lustie Maye,
>   Through glaidness of this Lustie Maye."
>
>   Scott

Scott also printed in St. Andrews several other books, among these being Archibald Hamilton's "Catechisme," which contains an oblong woodcut of Scott's device, rudely representing Hercules with a club in the act of striking a centaur. This work was printed in 1552 at the expense of John Hamilton, Archbishop of St. Andrews, and was a small quarto of about 200 pages, having the following full title: "The Catechisme. That is to say, ane commoun and catholik instructioun of the christin people in materis of our catholik faith and religioun, quhilk na gud christin man or woman sud misknaw: Set furth be the maist reuerend father in God Johne Archbischop of Sanct Androus, Legatnait and Prymat of ye kirk of Scotland, in his provincial counsale haldin at Edinburgh the xxvi. day of Januarie, the zeir of our Lord 1551, with the aduise and counsale of the bischoppis and uthir prelatis, with doctours of Theologie and Canon law of the said realme of Scotland present for the tyme." . . . "Agane reasone na sober man, agane scripture na christin man, agane ye kirk na peaceabil or quiet man will judge, or hald opinioun." Hill Burton says, "The authors of this manual of religious instruction to the laity had no benefit from the celebrated Catechism of the Council of Trent, which was not issued till a

later

later time. The Scots work had the advantage of appearing in a shape to be read by the people, instead of affording a mere aid to the clergy in the expositions they were told to make in the vernacular."*

George Chalmers, who made the productions of Scott's press, and particularly his editions of Lyndsay, a critical study, came to the conclusion that the printer had departed in many cases from his "copy," and believed him to have been an Englishman from his having Anglicised a number of the expressions and the spelling of many of the words. Great liberties appear to have been taken in this way with the original MS. of the Catechism, one of the most curious being on the page where we find "The Prayer of our Lord in Latyne," and below it, "The Same Prayer of our Lord *in Inglis*." This is, indeed, a singular heading to a very fair interpretation of the Lord's Prayer *in Scottis*. Hamilton's Catechism has been confounded by some writers with what was commonly called the "Twopenny Faith," a small work of four pages, issued by the authority of the Provincial Synod in 1558-59. This book was intended to be read as

a

---

* A copy of Hamilton's Catechism was sold some years ago for £148.

a preparation for receiving the sacrament of the Eucharist, supplying what in later times has been called "A Companion to the Altar," and it thus began with an exposition of the dogma of the real presence. It was looked upon with much scorn by the Reformers, and was spoken of by Knox as the "Twopenny Faith."

The fifth Parliament of Queen Mary, held at Edinburgh on 1st February 1551–52, passed an Act which furnishes some insight into the variety and character of the writings then issuing from the press and strongly influencing the public mind. The Act was as follows: "Prenters suld prent na thing without license. Item, For-sa-meikle as there is diverse Prenters in this Realme, that dailie and continuallie prentis buikes concerning the Faith, ballattes, sanges, blasphemationes, rimes, alsweill of Kirk-men, as Temporal, and vthers Tragedies, alsweill in Latine, as in Englis toung, not seene, viewed, and considdered be the Superioures, as apperteinis to the defamation and sclander of the Lieges of this Realme, and to put ordour to sic inconuenientes: it is devised, statute, and ordained be the Lord Gouernour, with aduise of the three Estaites of Parliament: That na Prenter presume, attempt, or tak vpone hande to prent ony bukis, ballattes, sangis, blasphematiounis, rymes or tragedies,

gedies, outhir in Latine, or Englis toung, in ony tymes to cum, vnto the tyme the samin be sene, viewit, and examit be sum wyse and discreit persounis depute thairto be the Ordinares quhat-sumevir, and thaireftir ane licensc had and obtenit fra our Soveraine Ladie, and the Lord Governour, for imprenting sic buikes vnder the pain of confiscatioun of all the Prentaris gudis, and banisshing him of the Realme for ever."

Scott returned to Edinburgh again, after being some years at St. Andrews, and resumed the work of printing. Among his productions after his return may be mentioned the following: "The Tragedie of the Vmquhile maist Reuerend Father Dauid be the Mercy of God, Cardinall Archibyschope of Sanctandrous, &c. Compilit be Schir Dauid Lyndesay of Mont, king of arms." At the foot of this title is Scott's device of Hercules and the Centaur. It was probably owing to Scott's issuing this work in 1558, without receiving license according to the Act of February 1551–52, that he was shortly after summoned before the Privy Council "for his demerits and faultes," a summons which by some means or other he seems to have evaded.

Scott again got into serious trouble with the authorities for issuing some time after the following-

ing

Printing in Edinburgh.

ing book: "The Last Blast of the Trompit of Godis worde aganis the vsurpit auctoritie of Ione Knox and his Calviniane brether, intrudit Pre-

SIXTEENTH CENTURY PRINTING-OFFICE.

cheouris &c. Put furth to the Congregatioun of the Protestantis in Scotlande, be Niniane Winzet, ane Catholik priest, borne in Renfrew. At the desyre and in the name of his afflictit Catholike Brether

Brether of ye inferiour ourdoure of Clergie, and laic men. *Vir impius procaciter obfirmat vultum suum: qui autem rectus est, corrigit viam suam.* Proverb. 21. Edinburgi vltimo Iulii 1562." This work is a Black-letter quarto, of which only five leaves are left in the only copy known. Niniane Winzet, the author, was schoolmaster in Linlithgow, and was among the most able as well as most active of the Roman Catholics in Scotland at the time of the Reformation. Even after the suppression of Popery in the kingdom, he ventured to publish in Edinburgh several works which were exceedingly distasteful to the feelings of the Reformers. The publication by Scott in May 1562 of one of these, "Certane Tractatis for Reformatioun of Doctryne and manneris," had greatly incensed the Reformers, who, upon learning that the "Last Blast" was in the printer's hands, took violent measures to put an end to his proceedings; and the magistrates of the city, with their officers, broke into the printing-house, arrested Scott, and put him in prison. The sheets of the work were seized, and the printing materials confiscated. But the author himself, who seems to have been on the premises at the time, and whose custody the Reformers chiefly desired, escaped in disguise, and made his way to Flanders.

How long Scott was kept in confinement is not known, or how he passed the remaining years of his life, but we next hear of him in 1568, engaged in printing the first complete edition of the works of Sir David Lyndsay for Henrie Charteris, a merchant and burgess of Edinburgh, who shortly after took up the trade of printing on his own account, and continued to exercise it successfully for many years. The imprint on this edition of Lyndsay reads: "Newlie imprentit be Iohne Scot, at the expensis of Henric Charteris: and are to be sauld in his buith, on the north syde of the gait, aboue the trone. *Cum priuilegio regali.*"

The art of printing, contributing, as it did, to the diffusion of knowledge and of liberal opinions, had ere this become an object of jealousy to the Church as well as to the State, and the General Assembly, in 1563, took the press almost entirely under its direction, prohibiting all books concerning religion to be printed, till the printers had obtained, not only license as formerly decreed from the civil magistrates, but also the approbation of the Church. Although an exclusive privilege was, by royal patent, occasionally bestowed on printers of vending or reprinting for a limited period those books which they had published, yet the occupation appears at this time still to have been by no
means

means profitable; for even the King's printer, who was also printer to the Church, was so distressed in circumstances as to be obliged repeatedly to implore and receive aid from the Church, and he at last received in March 1569-70 an annual salary of £50 from it, on account of his poverty and the great expense he had incurred in purchasing types. The printer to the King so aided was Robert Lekprevik, who was in business at the same time as John Scott; but what were then the privileges conferred on him or the precise value of the royal appointment, has never yet been satisfactorily ascertained. The tenement where Lekprevik had his workshop is not known, but it appears to have been somewhere about the eastern nook of the old town, near Netherbow Port.

One noteworthy book printed in 1560 by Lekprevik may be mentioned here: "The Confessione of the fayht and doctrin beleued and professed by Protestantes of the Realme of Scotland exhibited to the estates of the sam in parliament and by thare publict votes authorised as a doctrin grounded upon the infallable wourd of God. Matth. 24. And this glaid tydinges of the kingdom shalbe preached throught the hole world for a witnes to all nations and then shal the end cum. Imprented at Edinburgh be Robert Lekprewik. *Cum priuilegio,*

legio, 1561." The book is thus prefaced: "The estates of Scotland with the inhabitantes of the sam professing Christ Jesus and his holy euangell. To their naturall cuntre men, and to all others realmes and nations, professing the sam Christ Jesus with them, wyshe grace mercy and peace from God the father of our Lord Jesus Christ with the spirite of righteous iudgement for Saluation." On the last leaf of the book are these words: "From Edinburghe, 17. Augusti, 1560. These actes and articles ar red in the face of Parliament, and ratified by the thre estatis."

In February 1565, Lekprevik obtained a letter under the Privy Seal, authorising him to print "The Actis and Constitutionis of Parliament maid be the rycht excelent princes Marie quene of Scottis," and also the Psalms of David in "Scottis metir" for a period of seven years. A similar license was given him on January 14, 1567–68, for twenty years, of which license the following sentence forms part: "Thairfore Licencand and gevand to Robert Lekprevik Imprentar in Edinburgh priuilege and full power to imprent all and quhatsumever actis workis volumis and utheris necessaris alsweile in latine as in inglische for the weill and commoditie of the leiges thairof. And als all sic thingis as tendis to the glorie of God." This

This license was renewed on the 14th April 1568, and giving also an exclusive right to print "Ane buik callit ye Inglis Bybill imprentit of before at Geneva;" and yet neither Bible nor Psalm-book in "Scottis metir" ever issued from Lekprevik's press, although his other works are neither scarce nor unknown. It may be interesting to quote here the first official license to print the Bible in Scotland, and to some it will no doubt appear strange that, so far as regards the text of the Old and New Testaments, and the metrical Psalms, similar licenses are still required by printers in Scotland.

License to Lekprevik to Print the "Inglis Bibill," *April* 14, 1568.

"Ane Letter maid with awise of my Lord Regent To Robert Lekprevik our Soverane Lordis imprentare Givand grantand and committand to him full licence priuelege and power To imprent all and haill ane buke callit the Inglis bybill imprentit of before at Geneva And that continuallie induring the space of tuenty zeiris nixt following the dait heirof Chargeing all and sindrie imprentaris writtaris and utheris his hienes liegis within this realme That nane of thame tak upoun hand to imprent or caus be imprentit be quhatsumever persoun or persounis within this realme in ony tyme heireftir induring the said space under the panis of confiscatioun thairof The said buke callit the Inglis bibill viz. samony as salhappin

happin to be imprentit and payment of the soume of twa hundreth pundis money of this realme &c At Glasgw the fourtene day of Aprile The zeir of God In v^c lxviij zeiris."

Lekprevik's license of January 1567–68 empowered him also to print exclusively the "buikes callit 'Donatus pro Pueris,' 'Rudiments of Pelisso,' togedder with the gramer to be set furth callit the general gramer to be usid within scolis of this realme for erudition of the zouth."* Lekprevik appears to have gone afterwards for a time to St. Andrews, and several books with "Imprentit at Sanctandrois be Robert Lekprevik" are noted under the date of 1572 in Ames' "Typographical Antiquities."

The press was not likely to be a friend to the arbitrary Regent Morton, and the Regent, therefore, was not a friend to the press; and on July 29, 1574, he induced the Privy Council to issue another edict, to the effect "that nane tak upone hand

---

* The "Donat" was a grammar by Donatus, a celebrated grammarian, who was the preceptor of Jerome, and lived at Rome about 354. The "Donat" was one of the first books printed by Caxton, and also by Fust at Mentz. By an easy transition, the Donat—the name by which the work of Donatus was commonly known—came to signify in those times the elements of any art.

hand to emprent or sell whatsoever book, ballat, or other werk," without its being examined and licensed, under pain of death or confiscation of goods. The repeated issue of similar edicts at different times shows that their provisions were either not very stringently carried out, or that the printers paid little or no attention to them. One instance, however, of Morton's stern dealing with those who in this way gave him offence may be here given; though it would appear that it was the authors alone who suffered in this case. In September 1579, Walter Turnbull and William Scott were taken into custody in Edinburgh for writing a satire against Regent Morton, enumerating his crimes, and particularly insisting upon his connection with the death of the late Chancellor, the Earl of Athole. Turnbull appears to have been well known as an able schoolmaster, and both he and Scott, a "notar," for their good-humour and knack of rhyming, were in great repute both with the gentry and the common people. Many interested themselves in their behalf, and when they were carried to Stirling to be tried, the King was "pestered" with petitions for their liberty. Morton, on the other hand—for he never knew how to forgive an enemy—managed the process with so "much heat and concern," and so much overawed the

the young King James VI.'s inclinations to mercy, that upon the last day of October they were both publicly hanged. "Whilke was thought a precedent, never one being hanged for the like before; and in the meantime, at the scattering of the people, there were ten or twelve despiteful letters and infamous libels in prose found, as if they had been lost among the people, tending to the reproach of the Earl of Morton and his predecessors." "Some people alleged that the King was never inclined to pardon these two poets, because Scott one day, before some company, reading the Stirling Articles, suddenly stopped when he was but halfway, and being desired to go on, said, 'We will what Morton wills, and that is all.' 'Nay,' said Turnbull, 'add the Queen of England too.' The satire here was obvious enough to those who had read the Articles, and indeed it is not unlikely that this jest helped the unfortunate authors to the gallows." The following incident, related by Calderwood, in all probability forms the sequel. At the fall of Morton, less than two years after, when he was taken prisoner for his alleged complicity in the murder of Darnley, and conducted to Edinburgh Castle, "as he passed the Butter Tron, a woman who had her husband put to death at Stirling for a ballad entitled 'Daff and

dow

dow nothing,'* sitting down on her bare knees, poured out many imprecations against him."

Whether as a cause or a consequence of the edict of 1574 is not very clear, but in the same year Robert Lekprevik fell into disgrace, and was confined for a time in Edinburgh Castle for publishing, without license, "Ane dialogue or mutuall talking betwixt a clerk and a courteour, concerning four parische kirks till ane minister, collectit out of thair mouthis, and put into verse be a young man quha did then forgather with thame in his jornay, to the reproach and slander of our Sovereign Lord's Regent," &c. There is no doubt, however, that Lekprevik now forfeited his license as King's printer, though he continued to print for some years after; and about the same time he thus lost the royal favour, the printing of the first Bible in Scotland was undertaken in good earnest by Thomas Bassandyne—a matter of personal enterprise on the part of this printer which forms an important era in the literary as well as the religious history of Scotland.

* "Sport, and be at ease."

CHAPTER IV.

Bassandyne and Arbuthnot.

THOMAS BASSANDYNE was a native of Scotland, and was educated at Antwerp, from whence he seems to have gone to Paris, and afterwards to Leyden, where he learned the art of printing. He returned to Edinburgh in 1558, when he joined himself to the party of the Lords of the Congregation, as the Reformers were then called, and at the same time began business as a printer, having, it is believed, taken up that formerly conducted by Lekprevik, who had removed to St. Andrews. Bassandyne's workshop is referred to in the imprint to the rare quarto edition of Sir David Lyndsay's poems, printed in 1574, while "dwelland at the Nether Bow," and appears to have been in a tall narrow tenement nearly opposite John Knox's house. This building is supposed to be the one repeatedly referred to in the evidence of the accomplices of the

the Earl of Bothwell in the murder of Darnley, an event which took place in the lifetime of this old printer. In the deposition of George Dalgleish, one of those executed for his share in the crime, it is stated that "eftir thay entirit within the [Nether Bow] Port, thai zeid up abone Bassyntine's house, on the south side of the gait, and knockit at ane dur beneth the sword slippers, and callit for the Laird of Ormistounes, and one within answerit he was not there; and thai passit doun a cloiss beneth Frier Wynd, and enterit in at the zet of the Black Friers."

Bassandyne printed a number of books, and as the press was now fully under the special protection and control of the dominant Reformed Church, which had been established on December 20, 1560, and was sorely jealous of any encroachment of the civil powers, he appears to have fallen under the Church's displeasure for two works which he issued in 1568. On the 7th of July in that year, the General Assembly " declared and fund, that Thomas Bassendie, printer in Edinburgh, printed ane book, intituled the Fall of the Roman Kirk, nameing our King and Soveraigne supreame Head of the primitive Kirk. Also, that he had printed ane Psalme Book, in the end whereof was fund printit ane baudy sang callit Wellcome Fortune ; whilk books he had printit

printit without licensc of the magistrat or revising of the Kirk: Therefore, the haill Assembly ordained the said Thomas, to call in againe all the foresaids books that he has sauld, and keep the rest unsauld untill he alter the foresaid title, and also that he delait the said baudy sang out of the end of the Psalme Book; and, further, that he abstaine in all tyme comeing from further printing any thing without license of the supreame magistrat, and reviseing of sic things as pertaine to religione be some of the Kirk appointit for that purpose." Whether it was Bassandyne's object to get the song into circulation under the shelter of the Psalm Book, or to promote the sale of the Psalm Book by the insertion of the song, does not appear; but no doubt he had to obey the Assembly's mandate as to its withdrawal. Bassandyne seems afterwards to have regained the favour of the Church, as the title of the following book which he published fully indicates: "CL Psalms of David, in English Metre. With the forme of prayers, and ministration of the Sacraments, used in the Church of Scotland. Whereunto, besydes that was in the former bookes, are also added sundrie other prayers, with a new exact Kalendar, for xvi yeres next to come. Printed at Edinburgh by Thomas Bassendyne, dwelling at the Nether Bow, 1575. *Cum privilegio.*"

It

It has been already noticed that while Lekprevik was printer to the King and the Church, he received an annuity of £50 from the Kirk to help him. This allowance was made on March 3, 1569-70, in these terms: "The Kirk having respect to his [Lekprevik's] povertie, the great expenses he has made in bying printing irones, and the great zeal and love he beirs to serve the Kirk at all tymes, has assigned to him ffyftie punds yearly, to be payit to him out of the thrids of the Kirk." In spite of this annuity and other occasional help to the printers generally, it still appears that the art was not a prosperous one in those troublous times, as Bassandyne found himself necessitated to take into association in his business a burgess of the city named Alexander Arbuthnot, a man with a better connection and of more means. Their partnership was evidently also entered into for the purpose of undertaking the printing of a Bible, and instead of the usual thick quarto, in which Bibles had hitherto been done, their idea was to do it in folio form, as being possibly more within the compass of their resources. Accordingly, in March 1575, "Alexander Arbuthnot, burgess of Edinburgh, presented to the General Assembly certain articles for printing of the English Bible; whereof, with the answers of the brethren, the tenor followeth:

"Anent

"Anent the godly proposition made to the bishops, superintendents, visitors, and commissioners, in this General Assembly, by Alexander Arbuthnot, merchant burgess of Edinburgh, and Thomas Bassanden, printer and burgess of the said burgh, for printing and setting forward of the Bible in the English tongue, conforme to the proof given and subscribed with their hands; it is agreed betwixt this present Assembly, and the said Alexander and Thomas, that every Bible which they shall receive advancement for, shall be sold in albis for £4, 13s. 4 pennies Scottis, keeping the volume and character of the saids proofs delivered to the clerk of the Assembly.

"Item, for advancement of the godly and necessary work, and furtherance thereof, and home-bringing of men, and other provisions for the same, the bishops, superintendents, and commissioners, bearing charge within this realm under written, viz. James, Archbishop of Glasgow, &c., have, in presence of the Assembly, faithfully bound them, and obliged them, and every one of them, that they shall travel, and do their utter and exact diligence, for purchasing of such advancement as may be had and obtained within every one of their respective jurisdictions, at the hands of the lords, barons, and gentlemen of every parish, as also with the
whole

whole burghs within the same, and shall try how many of them will be content to buy one of the saids volumes, and will advance voluntarily the foresaid price, whole, or half at the least, in part of payment, and the rest at the receipt of their books, and shall try what every burgh will contribute to the said work, to be recompensed again in the books in the prices foresaid. And so many as be content to the advancement of the work foresaid, that the said bishops, superintendents, and visitors, collect the said sums, and enrol the samen with their names, what every one of them gives ; which roll, subscribed with their hands, and money, shall be sent by them to the said Alexander and Thomas, betwixt and the last of April next to come, and shall receive, upon their deliverance of the saids sums and rolls, the said Alexander and Thomas's hand writ, to the effect they and their cautioners may be charged for the said books conform to their receipt.

"Item, That every person that is provided of old as well as of new, be compelled to buy a Bible to their parish kirk, and to advance therefor the price foresaid, and the said prices to be collected and inbrought by the said bishops, superintendents, and visitors, within each bounds and shire within their jurisdiction, betwixt and the last day of June. And

And because the said Act appertains and is expedient to be ratified by my Lord Regent's Grace, and the Lords of the Secret Council, and an Act of Council to be made thereupon, the Assembly ordains Mr. David Lindsay, minister of Leith, Mr. James Lawson, minister of Edinburgh, and Alexander Hay, Clerk of Council, to travel with his Grace and their Lordships, for the obtaining the same, together with the privilege of the said Alexander and Thomas for imprinting of the said work.

"The Kirk ordains the said Mr. James and Mr. David to travel with Mr. Andrew Polwart and Mr. George Young, or any of them, for correcting of the said Bible, and to appoint a reasonable gratitude therefor at the cost of the said Alexander and Thomas.

"Item, The Kirk hath promised to deliver the authentick copy which they shall follow, to them betwixt and the last day of April.

"Item, for reforming [performing] of the said work by the said Alexander and Thomas, they have found cautioners, Archibald Seinzeour and James Norvell, burgess of Edinburgh, with themselves conjunctly and severally, that they shall deliver so many as they shall deliver advancement for perfecting of the said work, which shall be (God willing) betwixt and the last of March, the year

year of God 1576 years; and the said Alexander and Thomas are bound and obliged to relieve them.

Sic subscrib^r

  Alex. Arbuthnot, with my hand.
  Archibald Seinzeour.
  James Norvell, with my hand.
  Thomas Bassanden, with my hand."

The General Assembly gave favourable answer to the proposals, and appointed several persons "to oversee every book before it be printed, and likewise to oversee the labours of others that have travelled therein, to be given in to the printing betwixt and the last of April." The Government, under the Regent Morton, also gave a favourable ear to the project, and the Privy Council, seeing that "the charge and hazard of the wark will be great and sumptuous," decreed that each parish in the kingdom should advance £5 as a contribution, to be collected under the care of the said officers of the Church; £4, 13s. 4d. of this sum being considered as the price of a copy of the impression, to be afterwards delivered, "weel and sufficiently bund in paste or timmer," and the remaining 6s. 8d. as the expense of collecting the money. The money was to be handed over to Alexander Arbuthnot

Arbuthnot before the first of July next. The Bible was thus, in fact, a present from the people to their respective places of worship; and as a

BOOKBINDING IN SIXTEENTH CENTURY.

proof of their zealous desire, it deserves to be recorded that in most instances the money was furnished about three years before the Bibles were delivered.

delivered. Arbuthnot and Bassandyne, on their parts, bound themselves to execute the work under certain penalties, and respectable men came forward as their sureties to the Privy Council. Those who stood for Arbuthnot were David Guthrie of Kincaldrum, William Guthrie of Halkerton, William Rynd of Carse, and James Arnot of Lentusche—all Forfarshire gentlemen, a fact which argues that Arbuthnot himself was originally from the same district.

At the next General Assembly in August 1575, Arbuthnot again made an appeal for further encouragement, in which he says: "Whereas it is not unknown to your Wisdoms, what great work and charge I have enterprised, concerning the imprinting of the Bible, for accomplishing whereof, your Wisdoms understood that the office of a corrector, his diligence and attendance therein, is most necessary; and therefore I humbly desire your Wisdoms to request my Lord Abbot of Dunfermline to licentiate Mr. George Young, his servant, whom I think most fit to attend upon the said work of correctorie, to concur and assist me during the time of my travell, to the effect that the notable work begun and enterprised may be consummat and perfected in all points. The charges and expenses of his travells I shall reasonably deburse

deburse conforme to your Wisdoms' discretion, so that the work may pass forward and be decent, as the honesty of the same requires; whereunto I require your Wisdoms' diligent answer. And in like manner it is not unknown to your Wisdoms that for the furtherance of the same godly work, tane in hand by me, the order is tane that the bishops, superintendents, and commissioners, should diligently travell for the collecting, inbringing, and execution of the charge of our Sovereign Lord's letters, direct to that effect. In consideration whereof I earnestly desire your Wisdoms to command and charge every ordinar within his jurisdiction to put the said letters to due execution, and make me to be paid conform to the tenor of the same; whereby the godly enterprise of the samine may take full effect with expedition. And becaus your Wisdoms sufficiently understand, that the concurrence of my Lord Feuar of Orkney, shall greatly help to the expedition of the said work within his Lordship's bounds, I humbly desire supplication and request to be made to the said Lord, that he would, within the bounds of his jurisdiction, cause obedience and payment be made, conform to the tenor of the said letters: whereby I your Wisdoms' servitor shall pretermit no kind of diligence, expenses, or possible power in me
lyeth,

lyeth, that so the said godly work may take full furtherance, to the glory of God and the weal of his Kirk." To this supplication, the General Assembly, having read and considered it, also gave a very favourable response.

We do not know what were the exact arrangements between the two partners, Arbuthnot and Bassandyne, but we find that Bassandyne brought over from Flanders one Salomon Kerknett to act as "composer" at 49s. of weekly wages. Having "guid characters and prenting irons," it was thought the work, "great and sumptuous" as it was, would go quickly and pleasantly on; but this hope was not destined to be realised, as the printers found it a more serious undertaking than they had expected, and had met with, as they said, various "impediments." These impediments may have arisen from scarcity of type, and the difficulty of procuring paper, as there was certainly no type-foundry in Scotland in those days, and the first mention of a native manufacture of paper is referred to February 1589-90, when James VI. was absent on his matrimonial visit to Denmark. At that date, Peter Groot Heres, a German, and sundry persons associated with him, proposed to set up paper-making in Scotland, under favour of certain arrangements which they sought from the

Privy

Privy Council; but there is reason to believe this design proved abortive, and that there was no further attempt at native paper-making till 1675,

PAPER-MAKING IN SIXTEENTH CENTURY.

when a manufactory was established at Dalry Mills, on the Water of Leith, near Edinburgh.*

---

* The manufacturing of paper was first introduced into England by John Tate, in the reign of Henry VIII., or

The Bassandyne Bible.

A formal license was obtained from the Privy Council in 1576 permitting the publication of this Bible, of which license the following is a copy:

"LICENCE TO ALEXANDER ARBUTHNOT AND THOMAS BASSANDEN TO PRINT BIBLES, *June* 30, 1576.

"Ane letter maid to Alexander Arbuthnet burges of Edinburgh and Thomas Bassindyne prentare and burges of the said burgh Gevand grantand and committand to thame licence and priuilege to prent and caus be imprentit set furth and sauld within this realme or outwith the samin Bibillis in the vulgare Inglis toung in haill or in partis with ane callindare to be insert thairin for the space of ten zeiris nixt and immediatlie following the first begynning quhilk was the xxvij day of Merche the zeir of God I$^{mv^c}$ lxxvj zeiris of the said volume fra thynfwrth to indure ay and quhill the full completing and furthrynnyng of the saidis ten zeires allanerlie with power &c. Dischargeing all and sindrie his hienes liegis of quhatsumeuir estait or degre thai be of alsweil to burgh as to land as alsua strangearis repairing within this realme That nane of thame tak vpoun hand at ony tyme eftir the publicatioun of this his hienes priuilege during the said space of

---

perhaps of Henry VII. John Spilman had a patent for making paper in the time of Queen Elizabeth. Some of Caxton's books are printed on paper which bears the same marks as that used by Fust, and was probably of German manufacture.—*Ames and Herbert*.

of ten zeiris To prent or cause be imprentit in ony carrecture or lettir translatioun or volume quhatsumevir sell or caus be sauld brocht hame or distribute to ony persoun or persounes (except with the consent of the saidis Alexander and Thomas) vnder the pane of confiscatioun nocht onlie of the saidis volumes quhilk sal happin to be sua fund with ony persoun Bot alsua that the persoun offendane and contravenan of the premisses or ony part thairof To pay the sowme of ane hundreth pundis sa oft as thai sall happin to be apprehendit thairwith The ane half of the said confiscatioun and soumes to be ressavit to oure soverane Lordis vse and the uther half to the saidis Thomas and Alexanderis vses And this priuilege to indure the foirsaid space Providing that thai sell the saidis bibillis to all oure souerane Lordis liegis according to the prices appointit viz. everie bibill for four pundis xiij s iiij d with all and sindrie fredomes commoditeis &c."

Immediately after receiving this license, on the 8th July 1576, the printers, owing to the "impediments," whatever they may have been, came again with their sureties before the Privy Council, and pled for nine months' further time to complete the work, obliging themselves, in case of failure, to return the money which had been contributed by the various parishes and persons throughout the country. This grace was duly extended to them. Further delays still occurred, and whatever may have

have been the cause, Bassandyne himself seems to have been in fault, for he was shortly after ordered to give up the printing-office altogether to Alexander Arbuthnot—an order which he at this time managed to evade. On the 5th January 1576–77 the work was still in hand, and we have then a complaint made to the Regent by "Salomon Kerknett of Magdeburg, composer of wark of the Bible," to the effect that Bassandyne had refused since the 23d of December bypast to pay him the weekly wages of 49s., which they had mutually agreed upon when Salomon was engaged in Flanders. Regent Morton, finding the complaint just, ordered Bassandyne to pay Kerknett his arrears, and to continue paying him at the same rate till the completion of the work. Six days later a more serious complaint was made by Arbuthnot, that Bassandyne would not deliver to him, as he had contracted to do, the printing-house and the Bible, so far as printed, "wherethrough the wark lies idle, to the great hurt of the common weal of the realm." The Regent having heard parties, and being ripely advised by the Lords of Council, ordered Bassandyne to deliver the printing-house and Bible before the end of the month.

Bassandyne is believed to have died early in 1579, and in July that year the first Bible printed in

THE NEWE TESTAMENT
OF OVR LORD IE-
SVS CHRIST.

Conferred diligently with the Greke, and best approued
translations in diuers languages.

GOD  SAVE

THE KING.

AT EDINBVRGH.
PRINTED BY THOMAS
BASSANDYNE.
M. D. LXXVI.

CVM PRIVILEGIO.

Reduced facsimile of New Testament title

in Scotland was finished and in circulation; and it shows that Bassandyne commenced with the New Testament, which bears his imprint on the title and the date of 1576; while that of the Old Testament bears the name of Arbuthnot and 1579. In the following month of August, Arbuthnot was made King's printer, and received power to print all works in Latin, English, or Scots, "tending to the glory of God and commonweal of this realm, he obtaining first special license thereupon;" and he had special license granted him at the same time to print and sell Bibles "in the vulgar Inglis, Scottis, and Latin toungis, with ane callendar," for ten years.

The gratification of the clergy on seeing the Bible produced at a native press found eloquent expression in the Dedication of the work by the General Assembly to the King: "Oh quhat difference," said these devout men, "may be seene between thir days of light, when almaist in every private house the buike of God's law is red and understand in oure vulgarie language, & that age of darknes, when skarcelie in ane haill citie (without the clostres of monks & freires) cud the buke of God anes be founde, & that in ane strange tongue of Latin not gud, but mixed with barbaritie, used & red be fewe, & almaist understand

stand & exponit be nane, & quhen the false
namit clergie of this realme, abusing the gentle
nature of your hienes maist noble gudshir* of
worthie memorie, made it an capital crime to be
punished with the fyre to have or read the New
Testament in the vulgar language; and to make
them to all men more odious, as if it had been the
detestable name of a pernicious sect, they were
called New Testamenters.† . . . . . We ought,"
they said, "with the most thankful hearts to praise
and extol the infinite goodness of God, who hath
accounted us worthie to whom He should open
such an heavenly treasure." The writers of the
Dedication took advantage of it also to give a little
praise to Arbuthnot, "as a man who hath taken
great pains and travel worthy to be remembered;"
and told likewise how there should henceforth be
a copy of the Bible "in every parish kirk, to be
called

---

* His grandfather, James V.

† One of the "Gude and Godlie Ballats," beginning *The Wind blaws cald*, has the following lines relative to the New Testamenters in those "times of ignorance" to which the writers of the Dedication refer:

> "Quha dois present the New Testament,
> Quhilk is our faith surely,
> Priestis callis him like ane heretike,
> And sayis, burnt sall he be."

called the Common Book of the Kirk, as the most meet ornament for such a place."

The sale of this first Bible printed in Scotland was rather forced, for the Privy Council enacted that each householder worth three hundred merks of yearly rent, and all substantious yeomen and burgesses esteemed as worth five hundred pounds in land and goods, should have a Bible and Psalm-book in the vulgar tongue, under the penalty of ten pounds. To carry out this enactment, one John Williamson was commissioned in June 1580 under the privy seal to visit and search every house in the realm, "and to require the sicht of their Bible and Psalm-buke, gif they ony have, to be marked with their awn name, for eschewing of fraudful dealing in that behalf." About the same time the Magistrates and Town Council of Edinburgh issued a similar proclamation, commanding all householders to have Bibles, under the pains contained in the Act of Parliament, and advertising them that the Bibles are to be "sauld in the merchant buith of Andrew Williamson, on the north side of this burgh, besyde the Meill Mercat."

It appears from the Privy Council Records that this searcher was not idle, for several persons "incurrit the payne of the act for not having ane bybill or psalme buik;" and yet this rigorous enforcement

enforcement of the decree compelling the lieges to possess themselves of Bibles seems rather inconsistent with the fact that Arbuthnot was very tardy in delivering the copies, though he had received payment for them three years before publication. Twelve months after the first issue of the Bible, the General Assembly, in July 1580, presented the following petition to His Majesty's Council: "That order be takin with Alexander Arbuthnot that the Bibles may be delyverit according to his receipt of money from every paroch, & to that effect that he & his soverties [sureties] may be commandit be letters of horning for delyverance thereof, & na suspensioun to be grantit without the samyn be delyverit."

Curiously enough, Arbuthnot's promotion to be King's printer in August 1579 proved rather damaging to his repute as a printer, as after this he became noted for his incorrectness, and when the General Assembly presented the petition of July 1580, it was very evident from some of its clauses that for some reason or other he had greatly lost favour. Notwithstanding the number of presses now established in the city, the Assembly seemed to think the nation very inadequately served in the way of printing: "Because there is gryt necessitie of a prenter within the countrie, and there

there is a stranger banished for religioun, called Vautrolier, quha offers to employ his labour in the said vocatioun, for the weill of the countrie, it will please your Grace and Counsell to tak order herein as your Grace thinks guid, and to give license and privilege to him to that effect, if it sall be thought expedient be your Grace and Counsell." His Majesty followed the advice of the Church in this matter more cordially than in many others, as he repeatedly employed Vautrollier as the publisher and printer of works which were either his own or sent forth under his authority. Among the many works of Vautrollier's press was the " Essayes of a Prentise in the Divine Art of Poesie," written by the King himself. The title-page has for vignette an anchor, with the words "Anchora Spei," and the following imprint, " Imprinted at Edinburgh be Thomas Vautroullier. 1584. Cum Privilegio Regali." He likewise printed about the same time an edition of the Confession of Faith, and "A Declaration of the Kings Majesties intention and meaning towards the last Act of Parliament." A change of politics about this time, arising through King James having assumed into his own hands the reins of government, precluded all hope of Knox's History being allowed to be printed in Scotland, and Vautrollier made an attempt to have it done in England ;

England; but after the work had nearly reached completion, the press was stopped. This appears from the following extract from Calderwood: "February 1586, Vautrollier the printer took with him a copy of Mr. Knox's History to England, and printed twelve hundred of them; the stationers, at the archbishop's command, seized them, the 18 of February; it was thought he would get leave to proceed again, because the council perceived that it would bring the Queen of Scots in detestation." Copies of this imperfect edition were allowed to go forth, and are occasionally to be met with.

Arbuthnot printed, about 1580, the "Buik of Alexander the Great," which was reprinted by Dr. Laing in 1831–34; the original title of the work seems to have been "The Avowis of Alexander." At least, Henrie Charteris, bookseller in Edinburgh, who died 29th August 1599, had in his stock of books, "xii Avowis of Alexander bund, att x^s the pece;" also, "nyne unbund, at vij^s the pece;" and in a previous inventory of Robert Gourlaw, bookbinder, 6th September 1581, there was a copy of the "Vowis of Alexander, valued at $viij^s$." The original work is a small quarto printed in Roman letter, and does but little credit to the accuracy or elegance of Scottish typography. In this work there are many inverted letters; in the first sheets small

small letters were much used at the beginning of proper names, and in some cases several words are altogether illegible, owing to carelessness in printing, while other words are often separated or run together to accommodate the breadth of the page. The first edition of Buchanan's History was printed by Arbuthnot in 1582 in folio, "with many an error," says George Chalmers, "in every page." This work was done, fuller and more correctly, at Geneva in the following year; but the best edition is said to be that published at Leyden in 1725, in 2 vols. 4to, under the care of Ruddiman and Grenovius, on the basis of a previous folio edition of 1715, exclusively edited by Ruddiman. Arbuthnot died on the 1st September 1585.*

CHAPTER

---

* Arbuthnot the printer has been confounded by some with the Alexander Arbuthnot who, at the same period, was Principal of King's College, Aberdeen, and Moderator of the General Assemblies at Edinburgh in 1573 and 1577, and who was pronounced by James Melville to be "one of the most learned men of whom Europe could at that time boast." Chalmers, however, in his "Life of Ruddiman," thinks that, as Arbuthnot the printer is designated a "burgess of Edinburgh," he could not be the same person as Principal Arbuthnot. The point was settled beyond dispute by the discovery of the printer Arbuthnot's will, printed in the second volume of the "Bannatyne Miscellany." Principal Arbuthnot died at Aberdeen in 1583.

CHAPTER V.

The Bassandyne Bible.

HE following is the full title of the first Bible printed in Scotland: "The Bible and Holy Scriptvres conteined in the Olde & Newe Testament, Translated according to the Ebrue & Greeke, & conferred with the beste translations in diuers languages. With most profitable annotations vpon all the hard places of the Holy Scriptvres & other things of grete importance, mete for the godly Reader. God save the King. Printed in Edinbrvgh, Be Alexander Arbuthnot, Printer to the Kingis Maiestie, dwelling at ye Kirke of feild. 1579. *Cum gratia et privilegio regiae majestatis.*" The Bible was of double foolscap folio size, or about thirteen inches in height by nine in breadth, and the type used is what

Repent betime. The song of The soule immortal.

thou knowest not the worke of God that worketh all.

6 In the morning sowe thy sede, and in the euening let not thine hand rest: for thou knowest not whether shal prosper, this or that, or whether bothe shalbe alike good.

7 Surely the light is a pleasant thing: and it is a good thing to the eyes to se þ sunne.

8 Thogh a man liue manie yeres, (and) in them all he reioyce, yet be shal remember the daies of darkenes, because thei are manie, all that cometh is vanitie.

9 Reioyce, ô yong man, in thy youth, & let thine heart chere thee in the dayes of thy youth: & walke in the waies of thine heart, and in the sight of thine eyes: but knowe that for all these things, God wil bring thee to iudgement.

10 Therefore take awaye grief out of thine heart, and cause euil to departe from thy flesh: for childehode and youth (are) vanitie.

CHAP. XII.

1 Remember now thy Creator in the daies of thy youth, whiles the euil daies come not, nor the yeres approche wherein thou shalt say, I haue no pleasure in them:

2 Whiles the sunne is not darke, nor the light, nor the moone, nor the starres, nor clovdes returne after the raine:

3 When the kepers of the house shal tremble, and the strong men shal bowe them selues, and the grinders shal cease, because thei are fewe, and they waxe darke that loke out by the windowes:

4 And the dores shalbe shut withoutby the base sounde of the grinding, and he shal rise vp at the voyce of the birde: & all the daughters of singing shalbe abased.

5 Also they shalbe afraied of the hie thing and feare (shalbe) in the waye, and the almonde tre shal florish, & the grashopper shalbe a burden, and concupiscence shalbe driven away: for man goeth to the house of his age, and the mourners go about in the streete.

6 Whiles the siluer corde is not lengthened nor the golden ewer broken, nor the pitcher broken at the well, nor the whele broken at the cisterne.

7 And dust returne to the earth as it was, & the spirite returne to God that gaue it.

8 Vanitie of vanities, saith the Preacher, all is vanitie.

9 And the more wise the Preacher was, the more he taught the people knowledge, & caused them to heare, & searched forthe, and prepared manie parables.

10 The Preacher soght to finde out pleasant wordes, & an vpright writing, (euen) the wordes of trueth.

11 The wordes of the wise are like goades, and like nailes fastened by the maisters of the assemblies, (which) are giuen by one pastour.

12 And of other things besides these, my sonne, take thou hede: for there is none end in making manie bokes: and muche reading is a wearines of the flesh.

13 Let vs heare the end of all: feare God & kepe his commandements: for this is the whole (duetie) of man.

14 For God wil bring euerie worke vnto iudgement, with euene secret thing, whether it be good or euil.

AN EXCELLENT SONG
which was Salomons.

¶ THE ARGVMENT.

In this Song, so pleasantly by mystike sense and comfortable allegories & parables describeth the perfect loue of Iesus Christ, the true Salomon & the King of peace, to the faithful Church or his Church which he hathe sanctified & appointed to be his spouse, holy, cleare and vnblame to perfection. So that, howe so diuers & deepe the mysterie be, yet the glorie thereof doeth the burden rouse vnto the bride, and his great and excellent benefites towardes her, he doeth setteth foorth of her pure beautie and great mutual and ardent desires of her. Also the respect he sheweth of the Church which in himself and with the loue of Christ desires to be more and more ioyned vnto him in loue, and not to be ioyful of her selfe but of such goodnes as he gives her.

¶ CHAP. I.
1 The Spouse both the end of spiritual communication of Christ with those between Iesus Christ and his Church. 5 The dissimilitude between the Church.

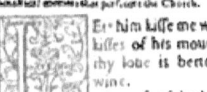

Let him kisse me with the kisses of his mouth: for thy loue is better then wine.

Because of the sauour of thy good ointments thy name (is as) an ointment powred out: therefore the virgines loue thee.

3 Drawe me: we wil runne after thee: the King hathe broght me into his chambers: we wil reioyce and be glad in thee, we wil remember thy loue more then wine: the righteous do loue thee.

4 I am

Reduced facsimile page of Bassandyne Bible.

what is known as a full-bodied pica, with the side and foot notes in bourgeois type. The book is signatured every twelve pages, and the pages themselves are in double columns, sixty lines in the column—the pages being numbered on the right hand only, the folios running from 1 to 503 in the Old Testament, equal thus to 1006 pages; while the New Testament has folios up to 125, equal to 250 pages, these being entirely independent of the introductory matter at the beginning, and of the various tables and indexes at end of the New Testament. The press-work is by no means so good, nor the type so regular, as that of many preceding books of the early Scottish printers; but no one can look even cursorily at the large folio volume without being struck with its comparatively modern appearance, and altogether this first Scottish Bible is creditable in a high degree to the skill and enterprise of Bassandyne and Arbuthnot. One feature is specially worthy of notice here—the fact that it is supposed to be one of the earliest Bibles in which Roman type was used throughout, Bibles previously having been in Black letter, and by the use of Roman type not only reduced in bulk, but also in price.

The Scottish printers of the time had little or no Greek or Hebrew type in their possession, and

Bassandyne,

Bassandyne, in his New Testament, contrived to find very clumsy Greek types for one solitary word in the note on Revelation xiii. 18; but his fount seems not to have comprehended all the letters in the Greek complement of type. The note says: "These greke characteres chi xi st [he means $\chi\ \xi\ \varsigma$] signifie 666; and this nomber is gathered of the small nomber λατεινος." Other books about the same period as the Bassandyne Bible show that, where words of these languages were required, blanks were left for them, and the words filled in with the pen after the sheets of the books were printed.*

The title-page is embellished with the royal arms, and "God save the King" by the side of the woodcut, notwithstanding the late reproof by the General Assembly to Bassandyne for considering and addressing the sovereign as the *head of the Kirk*. On the back of the title are the "Names and Order of all the Bookes." This is followed by a lengthy Introductory Epistle, in the Scottish dialect, to the "Richt Excellent richt heich and michtie prince Iames the Sext. King of Scottis." From this Dedicatory Epistle we have already quoted. Following this is "An Dovble Calendare,"

"to

---

* Greek type was first introduced into this country about 1524, and the first book certainly printed in that character was the Greek Delectus of Edward Grant in 1575.

"to vvit, the Romane and the Hebrew Calendare, conferred and compared the one with the other, meete for vnderstanding of the dayes, monethes and yeres mencioned in the Bible. And conteining many other profitable thingis not to be fund in other Calendaris." To these are subjoined " Rules for vnderstanding this dovble Calendare " by R[obert] Pont, a scientific ecclesiastic, who, with the leave of the Kirk, was appointed a Lord of Session, and died on the 8th of May 1608, at the age of eighty-one. To the " Calendares " are annexed some verses "On the incomparable treasure of the holy Scripture : "

"Here is the spring where waters flowe
    to quenche our heat of sinne ;
Here is the tree where trueth doth growe,
    to lead our lives therein.
	Esai 12. 3 &
	49. 10
	io. reul. 21.
	6 & 22. 17

Here is the Iudge that stints the strife,
    when mens deuises faile ;
Here is the breade that feedes the life,
    that death cannot assaile.
	Ierem. 33. 15 ;
	psal. 119. 160
	
	reuel. 2. 7, &
	22. 2
	psal. 119. 142,
	144
	Ioh. 6. 34

The tidings of saluation deare,
    comes to our eares from hence :
The fortress of our faith is here,
    and shield of our defence.
	Luk. 2. 10
	
	ephe. 6. 16

Then be not like the swyne that hath a pearl at his desire,	Matth. 7. 6

And

And takes more pleasure of the trough   2 Pet. 2. 22
    and wallowing in the myre.

Reade not this booke in any case,
    but with a single eye.   Matth. 6. 22
Reade not but first desire Gods grace,   Psal. 119. 27, 73
    to vnderstande thereby.

Pray still in faith with this respect   Iud. 20
    to fructifie therein,
That knowledge may bring this effect   Psal. 119. 12
    to mortifie thy sinne.

Then happie thou in all thy life,   Ios. 1. 8 / Psal. 1. 1, 2
    what so to the be falles :
Yea, double happie shalt thou be   Psal. 94. 12, 14
    when God by death thee calles."

To the verses, after a " Prayer for the true Vse of the Holy Scriptures," follows "A description and successe of the Kinges of Ivda and Iervsalem ; declaring vvhen and vnder vvhat kinges euery Prophete liued : And vvhat notable thinges happened in their tymes, translated out of the Hebrew." This again is followed by " An Exhortation to the studie of the holie Scripture, gathered out of the Bible." Then comes the Book of Genesis.

The Bassandyne Bible is one of the earliest editions of the Geneva version printed in Britain, and

is

is a verbatim reprint of the second Genevan edition published in 1561, which formed the "copy" furnished to Thomas Bassandyne by the Kirk. It has all the notes, and has facsimiles of the woodcuts and maps of the original copy, in all about thirty-eight, with the French terms attached to them, as *midi, orient, occident*, &c. Two blunders in the Genevan copy of 1561 were corrected in the Bassandyne, "Blessed are the place makers" for "peace-makers," in Matt. v. 9, from which error this Genevan edition is known also as the "Whig Bible;" and another in the contents of Luke xxi., "Christ condemneth the poor widow."

In the first edition of 1560, the supplementary words were printed in Italics, but in the second they were printed within brackets [ ], and this is the plan followed by Bassandyne. Evidently, however, when he commenced the New Testament, these types had not come to hand, for the brackets do not make their appearance till the Acts of the Apostles have been reached, as none appear in the Gospels. It is not unlikely this defect was one of the "impediments" of which the printers had complained. The Geneva Bible eventually became more popularly known as the "Breeches' Bible," from its rendering of the last clause of Gen. iii. 7, though this translation is not
peculiar

peculiar to it, as the same rendering is also used in the Wickliffite versions.

Of the various "Arguments" or summaries at the beginning of the books of the Bassandyne Bible, there are here given those of the first and the last books of the Scriptures :

"The First Boke of Moses, called Genesis.*

The Argument.

"Moses in effect declareth the things, which are here chiefly to be considered: First, that the worlde & all things therein were created by God, & that man being placed in this great tabernacle of the worlde to beholde God's wonderful workes, & to praise his name for the infinite graces, wherewith he hath endued him, fel willingly from God through disobedience: who yet for his owne mercies sake restored him to life, & confirmed him in the same by his promes of Christ to come, by whome he shulde ouercome Satan, death and hel. Secondely, that the wicked, vnmindful of Gods moste excellent benefites, remained still in their wickednes, & so falling moste horribly from sinne to sinne, prouoked God (who by his preachers called them continually to repentance) at length to destroye the whole worlde. Thirdly, he assureth us by the example of Abrahám, Izhák,

---

* This worde signifieth the beginning and generacion of the creatures.

THE SITVATION OF THE GARDEN OF EDEN.

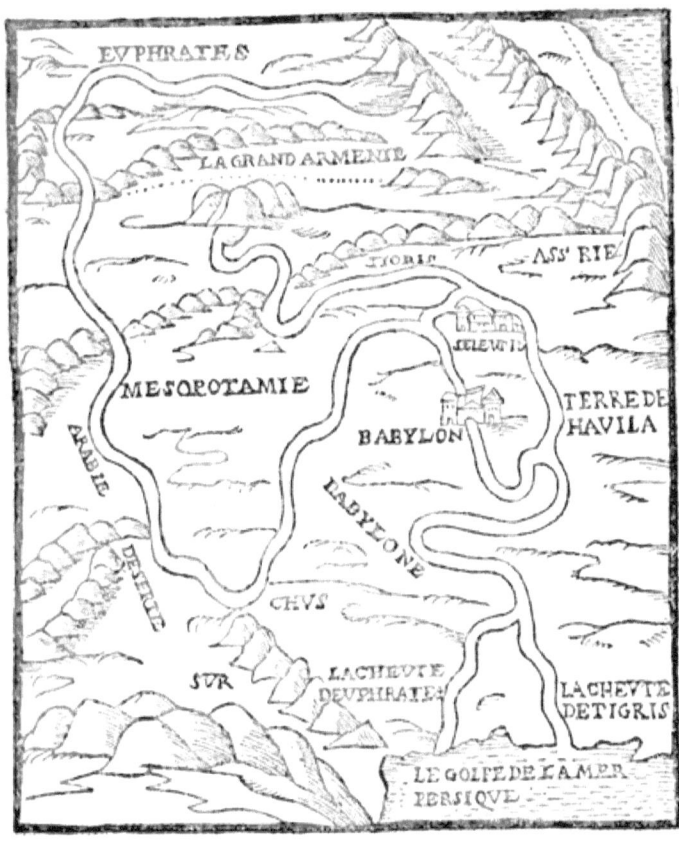

Facsimile from Bassandyne Bible.

"Because mention is made in the tenth verse of this seconde chapter of the riuer that watered the garden, we muste note that Euphrates and Tygris called in Ebrewe, Perath and Hiddekel, were called but one riuer where they ioyned together, els they had foure heades: that is, two at their springs, & two where they fel into the Persian sea. In this countrey and moste plentiful land Adam dwelt: And this was called Paradise, that is, a garden of pleasure, because of the frutefulnes and abundance thereof. And where as it is said that Pishón compasseth ye land of Hauilah, it is meant of Tygris, which in some countreis, as it passed by diuers places, was called by sondry names, as some time Diglitto, in other places Pasitygris, and of some Phasin or Pishon. Likewise Euphrates towarde the countrey of Cush or Ethiopia, or Arabia was called Gihon. So that Tygris and Euphrates (which were but two riuers, and some time when they ioyned together, were called after one name) were according to diuers places called by these foure names, so that they might seme to haue bene foure diuers riuers."—*Note to above Illustration in Bassandyne Bible.*

Izhák, Iaakób, & the reste of the Patriarkes, that his mercies neuer faile them, whom he chuseth to be his Church, and to professe his Name in earth, but in all their afflictions and persecutions he euer assisteth them, sendeth comforte and deliuereth them. And becaus the beginning, increase, preseruation and successe thereof might be onely attributed to God, Mosés sheweth by the examples of Káin, Ishmaél, Esaú and others, which were noble in mans iudgement, that this Church dependeth not on the estimacion and nobilitie of the worlde: and also by the fewenes of them, which haue at all times worshiped him purely according to his worde, that it standeth not in the multitude, but in the poore and despised, in the smal flocke and litle nomber, that man in his wisdome might be confounded, & the Name of God euer more praised."

"The Reuelation of Iohn* the Divine.

The Argument.

"It is manifest that the holie Gost wolde as it were gather into this most excellent booke a summe of those prophecies, which were writen before, but shulde be fulfilled after the comming of Christ, adding also suche things, as shulde be expedient, as wel to forewarne vs of the dangers to come, as to admonish vs to beware some, and encourage vs against others. Herein therefore is liuely set forthe the Diuinitie of Christ, & the testi-
monies

---

* Or, declared to Iohn.

monies of our Redemption: what things the Spirit of God alloweth in the ministers, and what things he reproueth: the prouidence of God for his elect, and of their glorie and consolation in the day of vengeance: how that the hypocrites which sting like scorpions the members of Christ, shalbe destroyed, but the Lambe Christ shal defende them, which beare witnes to the trueth, who in despite of the beast and Satan wil reigne ouer all. The liuelie description of Antichrist is set forthe, whose time and power notwithstanding is limited, and albeit that he is permitted to rage against the elect, yet his power stretcheth no further then to the hurt of their bodies; and at length he shal be destroyed by the wrath of God, when as the elect shal giue praise to God for the victorie; neuertheles for a ceason God wil permit this Antichrist, and strompet vnder colour of faire speche and pleasant doctrine to deceiue the world: wherefore he aduertiseth the godlie (which are but a smale portion) to auoide this harlots flateries, and bragges, whose ruine without mercie they shal se, and with the heauenlie companies sing continual praises: for the Lambe is maried: the worde of God hathe gotten the victorie: Satan that a long time was vntied, is now cast with his ministers into the pit of fyre to be tormented foreuer, where as contrariwise the faithful (which are the holie citie of Ierusalem, & wife of the Lambe) shal enioye perpetual glorie. Read diligently: iudge soberly, and call earnestly to God for the true vnderstanding hereof."

Of the marginal notes, forming a kind of commentary, and accounting in some measure for the great

great popularity of the Geneva version even long after the publication of King James's Authorised Version, there follow a few examples to show their general nature:

Exod. iv. 14.—"Thovgh we prouoke God iustly to angre, yet he wil neuer reject his."

Ruth i. 9.—"Hereby it appeareth y^t Naomi by dwelling among idolaters was waxen colde in ye true zeale of God, whiche rather hathe respect to the ease of the bodie than to ye comforte of the soule."

Psalm lxxxix. 12.—"Tabor is a mountaine vvestwarde from Ierusalem, & Hermon eastwarde: so the prophet signifieth y^t all partes and places of the worlde shal obey Gods power for the deliuerance of his Church."

Romans vi. 5.—"The greke worde meaneth, that we growe vp together w^t Christ, as we se mosse, yuie, mistaltow or such like growe vp by a tre, and are nourished with the ioyse thereof."

Romans ix. 15.—"As the onelye wil & purpose of God is the chief cause of election and reprobation: so his fre mercie in Christ is an inferior cause of saluation and the hardening of the heart an inferior cause of damnation."

Revelation

Revelation ix. 3.—"Locustes are fals teachers, heretikes, and worldelie subtil Prelates, with Mõkes, Freres, Cardinals, Patriarkes, Archebishops, Bishops, Doctors, Batchelors, and masters which forsake Christ to mainteine fals doctrine."

The following are two of the verses with the notes attached to which King James, in settling the arrangements for the preparation of the Authorised Version of 1611, objected as "very partial, untrue, seditious, and savoring too much of dangerous and traitorous deceits :"

Exod. i. 19.—"And the midwiues answered Pharaóh, Because the Ebrewe ^g women [are] not as the women of Egypt: for thei are liuely, & are deliuered yer the midwife come at them."

> "^g Their disobedience herein was lawful, but their dissembling euil."

2 Chron. xv. 16.—"¶ And King Asá deposed Maacháh [his] ⁱ mother frō her regencie, because she had made an idole in a groue: and Asá brake downe her idole, & stamped it, and burnt it at the broke Kidrón."

> "ⁱ Or grandmother: and herein he shewed that he lacked zeale : for she oght to haue dyed both by the

the couenãt, and by ye Lawe of God, but he gaue place to foolish pitie, & wolde also seme after a sorte to satisfie the Lawe."

The following are a selection of passages from the Bassandyne Bible:

Genesis iii. 1–7.

1. Now the serpent was more ^a subtil then anie beast of the field, which ye Lord God had made: and he ^b said to the woman, Yea, hathe God in dede said, Ye shall not eat of euerie tre of the garden?

2. And the woman said vnto the serpent, We eat of the frute of the trees of the garden,

3. But of the frute of the tre, which is in the middes of the garden, God hathe said, Ye shal not eat of it, nether shal ye touch it, ^c lest ye dye.

4. Then the serpent said to the woman, Ye shal not ^d dye at all,

5. But God doeth knowe, that when ye shal eat thereof, your eyes shalbe opened, & ye shalbe as gods, ^e knowing good and euil.

6. So the woman (seing that the tre was good for meat, and that it was pleasant to the eyes, & a tre to be desired to get knowledge) toke of the frute thereof and did eat, and gaue also to her housband with her, and he ^f did eat.

7. Then

7. Then the eyes of them bothe were opened, & ᵍ they knewe that they were naked, and they sewed figtre leaues together, and made them selues breeches.†

> ᵃ As Satan can change him selfe into an Angel of light, so did he abuse the wisdome of the serpent to deceaue man. ᵇ God suffered Satan to make the serpent his instrument and to speake in him. ᶜ In douting of Gods threatning she yelded to Satan. ᵈ This is Satans chiefest subtiltie, to cause vs not to feare Gods threatnings. ᵉ As thogh he shulde say, God doeth not forbid you to eat of the frute, saue that he knoweth that if you shulde eat thereof, you shulde be like to him. ᶠ Not so muche to please his wife, as moued by ambicion at her persuasion. ᵍ They began to fele their miserie, but they sought not to God for remedie.

GENESIS xlv. 26–28.

26. And tolde him, saying, Ioseph [is] yet aliue, and he also is gouernor ouer all the land of Egypt, and [Iaakobs] heart ⁱ failed: for he beleued them not.

27. And thei tolde him all the wordes of Ioseph, which he had said vnto them: but when he sawe the

---

† *Ebr.* things to girde about them to hide their priuities.

Genesis.

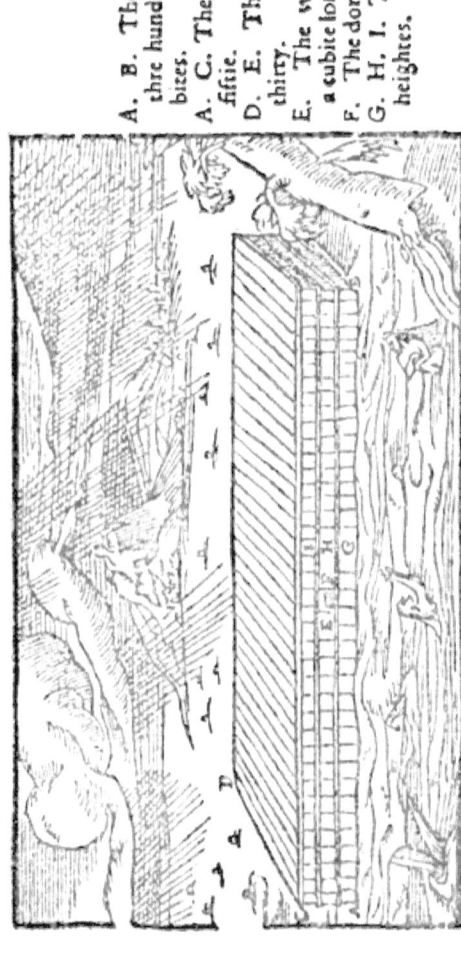

A. B. The length thre hundreth cubites.
A. C. The breadth fiftie.
D. E. The height thirty.
E. The windowe a cubite long.
F. The dore.
G. H. I. The thre heightes.

THE ARK.

Facsimile from the Lassandyne Bible.

the charets which Ioseph had sent to cary him, then the spirit of Iaakob their father reuiued.

28. And Israel said, [I haue] ynough: Ioseph my sone [is] yet aliue; I will go and se him yer I dye.

¹ As one betwene hope & feare.

Job xix. 25-27.

25. For I am sure, that my ᑫ Redemer liueth, and he shall stand the last on the earth.

26. And thogh after my skin [wormes] destroy this [bodie], yet shal I se God in my ʳ flesh.

27. Whome I my selfe shal se, & mine eies shal beholde, & none other [for me, thogh] my reines are consumed within me.

> ᑫ I do not so iustifie my selfe before the worlde, but I knowe that I shal come before the great iudge, who shalbe my deliuerer & Sauiour. ʳ Herein Job declareth plainely that he had a ful hope, that bothe the soule and body shulde enioye the presence of God in the last resurrection.

Isaiah xxvi. 19-21.

19. ᵗ Thy dead men shal liue: [euen] with my bodie shal thei rise. Awake, & sing, ye that dwell in dust: for thy ᵘ dewe [is as] the dewe of herbes, & the earth shal cast out the dead.

20. Come,

20. Come, my people: ˣ entre thou into thy chambers, and shutte thy dores after the: hide thy selfe for a very litle while, vntil the indignacion passe ouer.

21. For lo, the Lord cometh out of his place, to visite the iniquitie of the inhabitāts of the earth vpon them: & the earth shal disclose her ʸ blood, & shal no more hide her slayne.

> ᵗ He comforteth the faithful in their afflictions, shewing them that euen in death they shal haue life: and that they shulde moste certeinly rise to glorie: the contrarie shulde come to the wicked, as v. 14. ᵘ As herbes, dead in winter, flourish againe by the raine in the spring time: so they that lie in the dust, shal rise vp to ioye when they fele the dewe of Gods grace. ˣ He exhorteth the faithful to be pacient in their afflictions, and to waite vpon Gods worke. ʸ The earth shal vomit and cast out the innocent blood, which it hath drunke, that it may crye for vengeance against the wicked.

The Apocrypha portion has very few notes.

Ecclesiasticus xix. 1–6.

1. A laboring man that is giuen to drunkenes, shal not be riche: & he that contemneth smale things, shall fall by litle and litle.

2. Wine

2. Wine and women leade wise men out of the waye, and put men of vnderstanding to reprofe.

3. And he that companieth adulterers, shal become impudent: rottenness and wormes shal haue him to heritage, and he that is to bolde, shalbe taken away, and be made a publicke example.

4. He that is hastie to giue credit, is light minded, and he that erreth, sinneth against his owne soule.

5. Who so reioyceth in wickednes, shalbe punished: [he that hateth to be reformed, his life shalbe shortened, and he that abhorreth babling of wordes, quencheth wickednes:] but he that resisteth pleasures, crowneth his owne soule.

6. He that refraineth his tongue, may liue with a troublesome man, and he that hateth babling shal haue lesse euil.

2 MACCABEES xii. 44, 45.

44. For if he had not hoped, that thei which were slayne, shulde rise againe, it had bene superfluous, and vaine, to pray for the ª dead.

45. And therefore he perceiued, that there was great fauour laid vp for those that dyed godlie. (It was an holie, & a good thoght.) So he made

a reconciliation for the dead that they might be deliuered from sinne.

> [a] From this verse to the end of this chapter the Greke text is corrupt, so that no good sense, muche lesse certeine doctrine can be gathered thereby: also it is euident that this place was not writen by the holie Gost, bothe because it dissenteth from the rest of the holie scriptures, and also the autor of this boke acknowledging his owne infirmitie, desireth pardon, if he haue not attained to that he shulde. And it semeth that Jason the Cyrenean, out of whome he toke his abbridgement, is Joseph Ben Gorion, who hathe writen in Ebrewe fiue bokes of these matters, and in treating this place, maketh no mencion of this prayer for the dead, lib. iii. ch. 19, for it is contrarie to the custome of the Iewes, euen to this day, to pray for the dead. And thogh Iudas had so done, yet this particular example is not sufficient to establish a doctrine, no more than Zipporahs was to proue that women might minister the sacraments, Ex. iv. 25, or the example of Razis that one might kil him selfe, whome this autor so much commendeth, 2 Macc. xiv. 41.

Of New Testament passages we take the following:

JOHN x. 14–16.

14. I am the good shepherd, and [d] knowe mine, and am knowen of mine.

15. [e] As

15. ^e As the Father ^f knoweth me, so knowe I the Father: and I lay downe my life for my shepe.

16. ^g Other shepe I haue also, which are not of this folde: them also must I bring, and they shal heare my voyce: and there shal be one shepefolde, and one shepherd.

> ^d Christ knoweth his because he loueth them, careth and prouideth for them. ^e As the Father can not forget him, no more can he forget vs. ^f In that he loueth and approueth me. ^g To wit, among the Gentiles, which then were strangers from the Church of God.

ROMANS v. 12–15.

12. Wherfore, as by one man sinne entred into the worlde, and death by sinne, and so death went ouer all men, forasmuche as all men haue sinned.

13. For vnto the ^g time of the Law was sinne in the worlde, but sinne is not imputed while there is no Law.

14. But death reigned from Adam to Moses, even ouer them also that sinned not ^h after the like maner of the transgression of ⁱ Adam, whiche was the figure of ^k him that was to come.

15. But yet the gift is not so, as is ye offence: for if through the offence of one, many be dead,
muche

muche more the grace of God, & the gift by grace, whiche is by one man Iesus Christ, hathe abunded vnto many.

> ^g From Adam to Moses. ^h He meaneth young babes, whiche nether had the knowledge of the Law of nature, nor any motion of concupiscence, much lesse committed any actual sinne : & this may also comprehend the Gentiles. ⁱ Yet all mankinde, as it were sinned when thei were as yet inclosed in Adames loynes. ^k Which was Christ.

2 Cor. v. 11–15.

11. Knowing therfore the ^g terrour of the Lord, we ^h persuade men, & we ⁱ are made manifest vnto God, & I trust also that we are made manifest in your consciences.

12. For we praise not our selues againe vnto you, but giue you an occasion to reioyce of us, that ye may haue [to answere] against them, which reioyce in the ^k face, and not in the hearte.

13. For whether we be ^l out of our wit, [we are it] ^m to God : or whether we be in our right minde, [we are it] vnto you.

14. For the loue of Christ constraineth us : because we thus iudge, that if one be dead for all, then were ⁿ all dead.

15. And he dyed for all, that they which ^o liue,
shulde

In this figure foure chief points are to be considered. first that the Church of God is euer subiect in this worlde to the Crosse & to be afflicted after one sorte or other. The seconde, that the ministers of God following their vocation shal be euil spoken of, and murmured against, euen of them that pretend the same cause and religion that they do. The third, that God deliuereth not his Church incontinently out of dangers, but to exercise their faith and pacience continueth their troubles, yea and often tymes augmeneth them, as the Israelites were now in lesse hope of their liues then whē they were i Egypt. The fourth point is, that when the dangers are most great, then Gods helpe is moste ready to soucour: for the Israelites had on either side of them huge, rockes & montaines, before them the Sea, behinde them moste cruel enneemies, so that there was no way left to escape to māi Iudgement.

Facsimile from Bassandyne Bible.

shulde not hence forthe liue vnto them selues, but vnto him which dyed for them, and rose againe.

^g His fearful iudgement. ^h He proueth the dignitie of his ministerie by the frute and effect therof, whiche is to bring men to Christ. ⁱ By imbracing the same faith whiche we preache to others. ^k As they who more estemed the outwarde shewe of wisdome and eloquence, then true godlines. ^l As the aduersaries said, who colde not abide to heare them praised. ^m Our folie serueth to Gods glorie. ⁿ Therfore whosoeuer giueth place to ambicion or vaine glorie, is yet dead, and liueth not in Christ. ^o As the onelie faithful do in Christ.

1 Peter iii. 1–7.

1. Likewise let the wiues be subiect to their housbands that euen thei whiche obeye not the worde, may without ye worde be wonne by the conuersacion of ye wiues,

2. While thei beholde your pure conuersacion, whiche is with feare.

3. Whose apparelling let it not be outwarde, [as] with broyded heere, and golde put about, or in putting on of apparel.

4. But let the hid man of the heart be vncorrupt, with a meke and quiet spirit, which is before God a thinge muche set by.

5. For

5. For euen after this maner in tyme past did the holie women, which trusted in God, tier them selues, and were subiect to their housbands.

6. As Sarra obeied Abraham, and called him † Syr: whose daughters ye are, whiles ye do wel, not being ᵃ afraide of anie terrour.

7. Likewise ye housbands, dwel with them as men of ᵇ knowledge, ᶜ giuing honour vnto the woman, as vnto the weaker vessel, euen as they which ᵈ are heires together of the grace of life, that ᵉ your prayers be not interrupted.

† Or, master.

ᵃ But willinglie do your dutie : for your condition is not the worse for your obedience. ᵇ By nether keping them to streite, nor in giuing them to much libertie. ᶜ Taking care and prouiding for her. ᵈ Man oght to loue his wife, because they lead their life together, also for that she is the weaker vessel, but chieflie because that God hathe made them as it were felowe heires together of life euerlasting. ᵉ For they cannot pray when they are at dissencion.

The Bassandyne Bible contains also at the end of the New Testament several tables or indexes, of which there follow a few examples :

1. *A briefe*

1. *A briefe table of the interpretation of the proper names whiche are chieflie found in the Olde Testament, &c.*

Abél, mourning, the name of a citie, but Habél, the name of a man, doeth signifie vanitie, Gen. 4, 2.

Bacchides, one that holdeth of Bacchus, or a drunkard, 1 Macc. 7, 8.

Elymás, a corruptor, or sorceror, Acts 13, 8.

Iob, sorrowful, or hated, Iob 1, 1.

Shimshon, there the second time, because the Angel appeared the second time at the prayer of his father, Judges 13, 24.

A table of the principal things that are conteined in the Bible, after the order of the alphabet. The first nomber noteth the chapter, and the seconde the verse.

F.

Olde wiues Fables, 1 tim. 4, 7.
euerie one oght to proue his Faith, 2 cor. 13, 5.
the shield of Faith, ephes. 6, 16.
Christ prayeth for Peters faith, luke 22, 32.
the definition of Faith, ebr. 11, 1.
faith cometh by hearing, rom. 10, 17.
The apostles praye to haue their Faith increased, luke 17, 5.
learne to Feare God, deut. 14, 23.

the Feare of God is true wisdome, iob 28, 28.
¶ the Feareful must absent them selues from warre, deut. 20, 8.
the worthiest place at Feasts, matt. 23, 6.
feastes made at the shepeshearings, 2 sa. 13, 23.
¶ God teacheth to Fight, 2 sa. 22, 35.
the Finger of God, for his power, exod. 8, 19.
the First borne in the land of egypt, exod. 11, 4.
the First frutes, exod. 22, 29.
the First frutes perteined to the hie priests, nomb. 5, 9.
fishes cleane and vncleane, leuit. 11, 9.
¶ paul neuer vsed Flatterie, 1 thess. 2, 5.
¶ by the Folde is vnderstand the church, ioh. 9, 16.
our Forerunner, Christ, ebr. 6, 20.
Christ deliuered by the determinat counsel & Foreknowledge of God, act. 3, 23.
euerlasting Fyre prepared for the deuil, mat. 25, 31.

A perfite supputation of the yeares and tymes from Adam unto Christ, proued by the Scriptures, after the collection of diuers autors.

This contains the reckoning of "The summe of the yeres of the first age," in different paragraphs—

"From Adam to Noe.
From Noe to Abraham's departure to Chaldee.
From Abraham's departure to the Exodus.
From the Exodus to the first building of the Temple.
From the first building of the Temple to its re-building."

The

The following is the concluding paragraph of the "Suppvtation:"

"From the reedifying of the citie vnto the comming of Christ are 483 yeres, after this suppvtation or nombring. It is mentioned in the 9 of Daniel that Ierusalem shulde be buylt vp againe, and that from that tyme vnto the comming of Christ are 67 weekes, & euerie weeke is reckoned for seuen yeres. So 67 weekes amount to 483 yeres. For from the 32 yere of Darius vnto the 42 yere of Augustus, in the whiche yere our Saviour Christ was borne, are iust and complet so many yeres, wherevpon we recken, that from Adam vnto Christ are 3974 yeres, six moneths and ten dayes, and from the byrth of Christ vnto this present yere, is 1576.

"Then the whole summe and nomber of yeres from the begynning of the whole vnto this present yere of our Lord God 1576 are iust 5550, 6 moneths, and the said odde ten dayes."

The End.

Joshua, chap. i. vers. 8.

Let not this boke of the Lawe departe out of thy mouth, but meditate therein daye and night, that thou mayest obserue and do according to all that is writen therein: so shalt thou make thy way prosperous, and then shalt thou haue good successe.

The volume concludes with a table showing "The order of the yeres from Paul's conuersion shewing the time of his peregrination, and of his Epistles writen to the Churches."

CHAPTER

CHAPTER VI.

The Successors of Bassandyne.

AMONG the sixteenth-century Scottish printers contemporary with and following Bassandyne and Arbuthnot, besides Thomas Vautrollier, the refugee Huguenot, who is credited with having printed the first edition of Knox's "History of the Reformation," were John Ros (1574), Henrie Charteris (about 1582), Robert Waldegrave, and Robert Smith. The last named received a license from the King to print the following works, the titles of which show the books which were then probably the most popular in Scotland: "The Double and Single Catechisme;" "The Four Parts of Grammar, according to Sebastian;" "Select Epistles of Cicero;" "The Plain Donat;" the Psalms of Buchanan; "The Ballat Buik;" "The Fables of Æsop," &c. Among the books for which Smith received license was the following, and as it appears to have been very popular and often printed, the full title is given:

given: "Hier beginnis the sevin Seages, Translatit out of Prois in Scottis Meiter, be Iohne Rolland in Dalkeith, With ane moralitie eftir euerie doctouris Tale, and Siklyke eftir the emprice Tale; Togidder with ane louing and lawd to euery Doctour eftir his awin Tale: and ane Exclamation and outcrying vpon the Empreour is Wyfe, eftir hir fals contrusit tale. Edinburgh, Printit be Robert Smyth, dwelland at the Nether Bow. *Cum priuilegio regali.*"

There was also George Young, who, in September 1585, obtained full right to print whatsoever books had been included in the gift to Arbuthnot, including "all sic workes and volumes as sal be thocht meet and expedient to his Majesties estaitis and lordis of his priuie council to be set furth in the Latine, Inglis, or vulgar Scottis toungis tending to the glorie of God and common weill of this realme." In 1588 a work by King James, "Ane fruitfull Meditation on Rev. xx.," &c., and in 1589 another, "Ane Exposition of 1 Chron. xv. 25," &c., were both printed by Henrie Charteris, *cum privilegio regali*. Of these, and many other productions of the early Scottish printers, notwithstanding the largeness of the impressions, some have entirely disappeared.

However strange it may now appear, when we consider

consider that printers thus grew more plentiful, and that the demand for Bibles among the religious population of Scotland must have certainly increased, it is a fact that no edition of the Scriptures was issued in this country from the time of Bassandyne's Bible till 1610, the year before the publication of King James's Authorised Version. There are records, however, of editions of the Psalms and Catechisms for the Church of Scotland being frequently printed on the Continent, and imported into this country, as these were not used anywhere else; and also that one edition at least of the Scriptures was printed in 1601 at Dort for Scottish use. This latter work appears to have been done at the expense of Andro Hart and the heirs of Henrie Charteris, two Edinburgh printers, and the quality of the paper and the workmanship of the books printed abroad were generally such as to secure for them a preference at this time, although the Scottish press was then considered very respectable. In May 1590, for instance, John Gibson, the bookbinder to his Majesty, was empowered to print several books, such as the works of Sir David Lyndsay, the Dunbar Rudiments, the Seven Sages, and the Colloquies of Corderius. These he may have had printed in Edinburgh, but having in July 1599 received a
license

license to print the Psalm Book, it is evident that he had this done abroad, as in the preamble to his license it is stated that "John Gibson has, on his awin grit chargeis, and be his privat mean and devyse, causit imprent within Middleburgh in Flanders, ane new psalme buik in littil volume, conteining baith the psalmes in verse, as likewise the same in prose upon the margin, in ane forme never practisit nor devisit in any heirtofor, and tending gritly to the furtherance of the trew religion."

Andro Hart, to whom reference is made above, seems to have carried on the business of a bookseller on the north side of the Cross in the High Street of Edinburgh for a number of years, and his name appears on so many interesting title-pages, that he is really a notable man of his time. He and John Norton, an Englishman, also a bookseller, sent a petition to the Privy Council in February 1589-90, setting forth "what hurt the lieges of this realme susteinit through the scarcity of buiks and volumes of all sorts," and the high prices taken for these when brought from England. They, "upon an earnest zeal to the propagation and incress of vertue and letters within this realme, had, two years ago, enterprisit the hame-bringing of volumes and buiks furth of Almane and Germanie, fra the whilk parts the

the maist part of the best volumes in England are brought, and in this trade have sae behavit themselves that this town is furnist with better buiks and volumes nor it was at ony time heretofore, and the said volumes sauld by them in this country are als guid cheap as they are to be sauld in London or ony other part of England, to the great ease and commodity of all estates within this realme."

Many popular books must have been at this time imported from abroad, as it is said that in 1610 there were in circulation about thirty foreign editions of Buchanan's Psalms, nine or ten editions of the works of Sir David Lyndsay, some of these latter having been printed in France and some in England. The complaint of Hart and Norton now was that "John Gourlay, the customer" (that is, the farmer of customs), had laid hands upon the books which Hart and Norton were importing, and demanded that they should pay a duty. The petitioners referred to a like complaint formerly made by Thomas Vautrollier, printer, when "he obteinit ane decreet dischargeing the provost and bailies of this burgh and their customer fra all asking of ony customs for ony books sauld or to be sauld by him," and Hart and Norton only sought to be treated in like manner. The Lords unhesitatingly granted the prayer of the two booksellers.

sellers. In the course of a few years Hart appears to have severed his connection with Norton; and in 1597 Hart found it necessary again to petition the Lords of Exchequer against the customer's exactions, and the Lords repeated that they "declaris and ordanis that thair salbe na maner of custome or customes askit sutit or tane fra the said complenar for ony bukis or volumis alreddie brocht in or to be brocht in be him within this realme in ony tyme cuming. And therfoir ordanis the said John gourlay customar foirsaid and all vtheris customaris of Edinburgh present or that salhappin to be for the tyme as alsua all vtheris customaris of quhatsumevir burrowis and portis of this realme To decist and ceis fra all asking craving or suting of ony custome fra the said andro hart complenar foirsaid for ony bukis or volumis brocht in or to be brocht in or sauld be him within this realme in ony tyme cuming," &c.

Andro Hart printed another Bible in 1610, which was so much esteemed for its general correctness, that many subsequent editions bore upon their titles "conform to the edition printed by Andro Hart"—a very handsome one, printed at Amsterdam by Thomas Stafford, an Englishman, claiming this distinction; and similarly another so late as 1644. Hart's Bible, like that of Bassandyne,

dyne, was also in folio, and, though well adapted for general use, could hardly be obtainable by people in humble circumstances. This Bible has been described as an edition of the Geneva version; still it was not a reprint of Bassandyne's, or of that printed at Geneva in 1610. The Old Testament is indeed the same in both text and notes, but the New Testament is not from the Geneva, but from one published by Laurence Tomson in 1576, which, though not varying much in the text, has very different annotations in the margin. In this way it turns out that many of the verses which have marginal notes in Bassandyne's have none in Hart's, and, on the other hand, copious notes are often given by Hart where Bassandyne has none. The following is the full title of Hart's New Testament: " The New Testament of our Lord Jesus Christ, translated out of Greeke, by Theod. Beza. Whereunto are adjoyned briefe Summaries of Doctrine upon the Evangelists and Acts of the Apostles, together with the Methode of the Epistles of the Apostles, by the said Theod. Beza. And also short Expositions on the Phrases and Hard Places, taken out of the large Annotations of the foresaid Author, and Joach. Camerarius, by P. Los Valerius. Englished by L. Tomson. Together with the Annotations of Fr. Junius, upon Revelation

Revelation of St. John." There follows at the end two tables: the first, " Of the Interpretation of Proper Names, which are chiefly found in the Old Testament;" the second table is, " Of the principal things that are contained in the Bible, after the order of the alphabet."

It is curious that Hart published this book in the face of Robert Charteris, then printer to his Majesty, who had, in June 1606, received a special license for twenty-five years to print the Bible in the vulgar tongue; but the fact is, that, like Lekprevik, his predecessor in the office, he never published any edition of the Scriptures. Below the title of Hart's Bible is an engraving representing the passing of the Red Sea, which is encompassed with the words, " Great are the troubles of the righteous; but the Lord delivered them out of them all "—Psalm xxxiv. Under this again is the text: "'The Lord shall fight for you; therefore hold you your peace.' At Edinburgh, printed by Andro Hart, and are to be sold at his buith, at the north side of the gate, a little beneath the cross. Anno Dom. 1610." The Diocesan Synod of St. Andrews, in April 1611, recommended all ministers of the Church to urge upon their parishioners to " buy ane of the Bybles laitlie printed be Andro Hart," and the brother failing to follow out this
instruction

instruction was to pay at the next Synod a fine of ten shillings sterling. It is interesting to note that Andro Hart in 1614 published Barbour's "Bruce," and, about the same time, a small volume entitled "Mirifici Logarithmorum Canonis Descriptio, &c. Auctore et Inventore Ioanne Napero, Barone Merchistone, Scoto." This was a remarkable event, considering the many traits of bigotry and ignorance that distinguished the time, for in Napier's volume was presented a mode of calculation which has been of service ever since in the solution of all the great problems involving numbers which have presented themselves to the scientific studies of the race.

Hart also printed a volume in Black letter entitled "Ane Compendious Booke of Godlie and spirituall Sangs, collectit out of sundrie partes of the Scripture, With sundrie other Ballates, changed out of prophane sanges," which is believed to have been partly written by Wedderburn, the author of "The Complaynte of Scotland." Although the authorities tried several times to repress their circulation, yet these ballads were not only great favourites, but they had, in their day, also considerable influence on the life of the common people. One of these "blasphematiounis rimes" was the following direct hit at the Romish clergy, in which the spelling is modernised :

"With

"With hunts up, with hunts up,
    It is now perfect day;
Jesus our King is gone a-hunting,
    Who likes to speed, they may.

An cursed fox lay hid in rocks
    This long and many a day,
Devouring sheep, while he might creep,
    None might him shape away.

It did him good to lap the blood
    Of young and tender lambs;
None could him miss, for all was his,
    The young ones with their dams.

The hunter is Christ, that hunts in haste;
    The hounds are Peter and Paul;
The Pope is the fox; Rome is the rocks,
    That rubs us on the gall.

That cruel beast, he never ceased
    By his usurped power,
Under dispense, to get our pence,
    Our souls to devour.

Who could devise such merchandise,
    As he had there to sell,
Unless it were proud Lucifer,
    The great master of Hell?

He had to sell the Tantonie bell;
    And pardons therein was,
Remission of sins in old sheep skins,
    Our souls to bring from grace.

                                    With

> With bulls of lead, white wax, and red,
> And other whiles with green,
> Closed in a box, this used the fox;
> Such paultry was never seen."

Another remarkable book, published June 13, 1616, was a work called "God and the King," "shewing that his sacred majesty being immediately under God within his dominions, doth rightfully and lawfully claim whatsoever is required by the aith of allegiance," and was proclaimed as a book of instruction for youth in schools and universities, "whereby, in their tender years, the truth of that doctrine may be bred and settled in them, and they thereby may be the better armed and prepared to withstand any persuasion that in their riper years may be offered and usit towards them for corrupting of them in their duty and allegiance." Hart died in 1621, at an advanced age.

Following Hart, the progress of the printer's art may be briefly noticed till the time of Mrs. Anderson, one of the most remarkable of Bible printers, and among the names now will be found those of Thomas Finlayson and Robert Young.

Finlayson seems to have possessed the usual aptitude of the printers of those early times for getting into trouble with the authorities, as is shown

shown in the following incident. In 1607, Sir John Skene of Currichill, a Lord of Session, completed his "Regiam Majestatem" and "Quoniam Attachiamenta," treatises concerning the ancient laws of Scotland, and presented them to the Privy Council, who recommended the work to James VI. in a letter dated 15th March that year. The volume was afterwards presented to Parliament and ordered to be printed, for which purpose the learned author employed Thomas Finlayson. The expense of printing, and the remuneration to Sir John Skene, was evidently to be defrayed by contributions from the various burghs, as in April 1609 we find the magistrates of Glasgow called upon to make payment of £100 for this purpose. In September 1607, the author had some dispute with his printer about the work, of importance enough to come under the attention of the Privy Council. It was alleged that Finlayson, after *perfyting* the volume, "upon some frivole consait and apprehension of his own, without ony warrant of law or pretence of reason," maliciously refused to deliver the book to Sir John Skene, "but shifts and delays him fra time to time, with foolish and impertinent excuses, to Sir John's heavy hurt and prejudice." The Lords ordered Finlayson to deliver the book to its author within eight days, on pain

pain of being denounced rebel; and "wheras there is some little difference and question betwixt the said parties anent their comptis," a committee was appointed " to sort the same and put them to ane rest."

Robert Young had the honour of being printer to Charles I., and in 1633 he turned out the first edition of any part of the Scriptures, according to King James's Authorised Version, which was published in Scotland. This was only, however, the New Testament portion, and he issued two impressions, both of small size; and the number of copies of the second one is said to have been very limited, some of these having plates. This is believed to be the edition referred to in a remarkable letter contained in the Wodrow Collection of Manuscripts, and printed by Lord Hailes in his " Memorials and Letters." " That you may taste a little of our condition," says the writer, " I have sent you two of our own Scots Bibles, the New Testament only, wherein they have placed such abominable pictures, that horrible impiety stares through them. These come forth by public authority. Do you show them to such as you think meet." It is asserted in one of the charges against Archbishop Laud that he had brought these Popish pictures from foreign parts, and that

with

with his "good liking" they were bound up in English Bibles, which were called the Archbishop of Canterbury's Bibles. The number of plates in the original book is said to be seventy-four, most of them finely executed. The Edinburgh edition of 1633, in which in some instances they have been inserted, is printed in double columns, and bears a great resemblance to some London editions of the same period.

Young in 1637 produced a Book of Common Prayer or Scottish Service Book in folio, which was considered to be far superior to those executed in England at that time. Watson ("History of Printing," 1713) says of this Prayer Book, the merit of which apparently proved the printer's ruin in Scotland, "I have, with great Pleasure, view'd and compar'd that Book with the English one in the same Volume, printed about the same Time by the King's Printers in England: And indeed Mr. Young's Book so far exceeded the other, that there could be no Comparison between them. You'll see by That printed here, the Master furnish'd with a very large Fount, Four Sheets being inset together; a vast Variety of curiously cut Head-Pieces, Finis's, Blooming-Letters, Fac-totums, Flowers, &c. You'll see the Compositor's Part done with the greatest Regularity and Niceness in the Kalendar; and throughout

throughout the rest of the Book. The Press-Man's Part done to a Wonder in the Red and Black, and the whole printed in so beautiful and equal a Colour, that there is not any Appearance of Variation. But this Good and Great Master was ruin'd by the Covenanters for doing this Piece of Work, and forc'd to fly the kingdom." It appears from the letters of Archbishop Laud that Young must after this have resided in London, whence he transmitted types and instructions to his workpeople in Edinburgh. Charles I.'s "Large Declaration concerning the Tumults in Scotland" was printed in London by Young, his Majesty's then printer for Scotland, in 1639, at which time many tracts and pamphlets professing to be printed in Edinburgh bear the same name and designation.

The tumults referred to in Charles I.'s "Large Declaration" were the results of the attempts begun by James VI. to introduce the Episcopal service into Scotland, because it was thought dangerous to the English Church that a form of worship resembling that of the Puritans should exist in any part of the King's dominions. The same object was further carried on with greater zeal by Charles I.; and although the people were generally adverse to it, he had succeeded, after a visit which he paid

to

The Successors of Bassandyne.

to Scotland in 1633, in settling thirteen bishops *
over the Church, by whom he hoped to govern the
Scottish clergy as he did those of England. But
when he attempted in 1637 to introduce the new
Book of Common Prayer into the Scottish churches,
the spirit of the people could no longer be kept
within bounds. On the liturgy being opened in
the principal church in Edinburgh, the congregation
rose in a violent tumult, and threw their clasped
Bibles, and the very stools they sat on, at the
minister's head; and it was not till the people were
expelled by force that the worship was permitted
to proceed. It was found necessary by the Scottish state officers to withdraw the obnoxious liturgy
till they should consult the King, who, not dreading
any mischief, gave orders that it should be used as
he had formerly directed, and that the civil force
should be used in protecting the clergymen.

In connection with all this, we learn further
that "Mr. Andrew Ramsay and Mr. Henry Rollock, ministers in Edinburgh, were accused for not
buying

---

* These bishops were known as the Tulchan Bishops :
a *tulchan* being a calf's skin stuffed to induce the cow to
give milk, and the bishops being regarded by the Scottish
people as an invention of the lairds to get the rents out of
the Church lands, to which otherwise they had a difficulty
in establishing a right.

buying and using the Common Prayer Books at the King's command. They answer, it was contrary to the orders of their Kirk and their own consciences, and so would not use them. Followed another Council day, where there were convened about one hundred ministers, well backed with their nobles and gentlemen, who refused using the service books, as contrary to the constitution of the Kirk and worship of God, whereupon they offered public disputation, and so departed. Upon the first Sunday of October 1637, the provincial synod sat down in Murray: the Bishop of Murray desired the ministry to buy and use the service book, conform to the King's command, as all the bishops had done; so some bought, some took to be advised, and some refused. The bishops had caused imprint thir books, and payed for the samen, and should have gotten frae each minister four pounds for the piece." King Charles thus found it quite impossible to force observance to his commands in the face of a united people, represented by nobles, ministers, gentry, and burghers, who endeavoured to awe the King into an abandonment of the liturgy; and he used every means in his power to avoid such humiliation, which he believed would give immense force to the innovators in England. But the Scottish people, when they found

found him hesitating, bound themselves (March 1638) under a bond called the National Covenant, which was signed by a large proportion of the adult population, to resist their sovereign in every attempt he might make to bring in upon them the errors of Popery, for such they held to be the forms of worship and ecclesiastical government which Charles had lately imposed upon their Church.

In November the same year we read of Raban, a well-known printer in Aberdeen, issuing "diverse copies of a proclamation of the King against disobedient subjects, relating to a dispute between him and the General Assembly," and it must have been to this proclamation, or to the Declaration printed by Young in London, that the Covenanters wrote out an answer, called "The Remonstrance of the Nobility, Barons, Burgesses, Ministers, and Commons, within the kingdom of Scotland. Imprinted at Edinburgh by James Bryson, 1639. By the whilk they set down an answer to ilk particular reason contained in the King's proclamation, and that they had done no wrong in their haill procedure, and that any proclamation made in England, or sent down here to be proclaimed in Scotland, declaring them, and the most part of the body of the kingdom, to be rebels and traitors, was in itself null and unlawful, as done by the King upon information of wicked and seditious persons, seeking their own ends, without advice of council or parliament, who had special power in declaring matters of treason, and therefore had good reason to stay the publication of such illegal proclamations."

Specimen of Initial Letters in Bassandyne Bible.

CHAPTER VII.

Evan Tyler—The Andersons.

EVAN TYLER, the next printer who held the royal office in order of time, had been appointed jointly with Young in 1641, and he published in 1642 a neat Pocket Bible in two parts, and also in 1643 an octavo New Testament in Black letter. The largest size Tyler is known to have ever printed was an octavo in 1649, whilst he also furnished editions of the Scotch Psalms to be bound up with Bibles printed by Charles Bill in London, after the certified approval of these Psalms for public worship by the General Assembly in May 1650.* After the death of Young, Tyler became sole possessor of the royal appointment, but during the Civil Wars, according to Watson's "History of Printing," he basely deserted

---

* A facsimile of a title-page of Evan Tyler's Scotch Psalms is given on page 179, from a copy of a "Bill" Pocket Bible.

deserted his master's interest, and was in his turn obliged to fly when Charles II. was in Scotland in 1650, a sentence of forfeiture having been passed on him at Scone. On Cromwell gaining ascendancy in the North, however, Tyler assigned his patent to some London stationers, who sent down Christopher Higgins, with some other English printers. These carried on a business at Leith, which consisted chiefly in reprinting a newspaper called "A Diurnal of Some Passages of Affairs," first printed in London; they also issued some small books, said by Watson to have been very badly done. After the death of Higgins, the London stationers appointed a Scottish printer named Patrick Ramsay to oversee their printing-office, but eventually the establishment was broken up and sold to several booksellers in Edinburgh, who very soon divided and set up distinct houses.

The statement of Watson's History that Tyler was declared rebel by Charles II. in 1650 seems at variance with the fact that he printed at Edinburgh "A Declaration of the King's Majesty to his Subjects of the Kingdomes of Scotland, England, and Ireland," said to be "given at our Court at Dunfermline the 16th day of August 1650, and in the second year of our Reign." It bears to have been "printed by Evan Tyler, Printer to the King's Most

THE PSALMS OF DAVID
In Meeter.

Newly Tranflated, and Diligently Compared with the Original Text, and former Tranflations: More plain, fmooth and agreeable to the Text, than any heretofore.

Allowed by the Authority of the General Affembly of the Kirk of *Scotland*; and appointed to be fung in Congregations and Families.

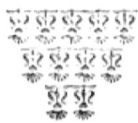

EDINBURGH

Printed by *Evan Tyler*, Printer to the King's moft Excellent Majefty, 1698.

Most Excellent Majesty, 1650." Spottiswood (Miscellany, vol. i.) also disputes Watson's accuracy on this point; and says: "During the Commonwealth, it was but natural to suppose that the existing powers would not employ a person who had permitted the Proclamations and official documents of Charles II. to issue from his press, and in the interval between the flight of Charles and his restoration, Tyler could not expect to receive any countenance from Cromwell; but after the Stuarts were restored to the throne of their ancestors, his truckling to the Parliament was overlooked, probably on account of his non-adherence to the Protector, and he was restored to the office of King's printer. How long he continued to hold that office has not been ascertained, but Proclamations by the Privy Council that issued from his press have been found, dated in 1664."

During the troubles, Robert and James Bryson made application for the appointment of royal printers, but were unsuccessful in their attempt, for evidently Evan Tyler printed both the Acts of Parliament and of the General Assembly for many years, thus showing that the services of the alleged renegade were considered by the dominant party more worthy of reward than those of the consistent Covenanters. However, as some small recompense, several

several books were given to the Brysons to print by the General Assembly. Among other works printed by Robert Bryson were two of the poetical lucubrations of William Lithgow the traveller. One of these was entitled: "The Gushing Tears of Godly Sorrow, containing the Causes, Condition, and Remedies of Sinne, depending mainly upon Contrition and Confession; and they Seconded with Sacred and Comfortable Passages under the Mourning Cannopie of Teares and Repentance." This small quarto was printed in 1640, "at the expense of the author," and dedicated to the Earl of Montrose, and affords a very favourable specimen of Bryson's typographical abilities.

In May 1650, the "new Psalm-books [the Psalms referred to above] were read and ordained to be sung through all the kingdom." This was the translation of the Psalms which is still used by the Church of Scotland and other Presbyterian congregations. It was based on a homely version produced originally in 1643 by Francis Rous, a member of the Long Parliament, who ultimately became Provost of Eton, and died in 1658. What was rather curious, Rous was at this time joined to the sectaries, against whom the Scottish Church entertained so bitter a feeling. It must be admitted that his version underwent great improvements in the

the hands of the committees of the General Assembly appointed for its revision. As now finally sent forth, it was in many respects most felicitous. The general strain and metre is that of the old homely ballad. It is occasionally harsh and obscure, has a few Scottish idioms, and sometimes requires an obsolete pronunciation to make out the prosody; yet, with all these obvious faults, it perhaps comes nearer to the simple beauty of the original than any other metrical translation.

After Tyler, about 1650, came Archibald Hyslop, a bookseller, who set up a printing-office with William Carron, an excellent workman. They brought new materials from Holland, and printed an edition of Thomas-à-Kempis, as well as other books. While the art seemed at this time about to revive, it received an almost mortal blow through the conferring of a monopoly of printing on Andro Anderson, by the administration of Charles II.— "an administration whose attention seems to have been divided between exalting the royal prerogative and gratifying their own rapacity, but seldom applied to a consideration of the welfare of the people."

Andro Anderson was the son of George Anderson, who, in 1638, introduced the art of printing into Glasgow, having been invited from Edinburgh by by the magistrates for that purpose, and it appears from the Council Records of the former city that he was allowed £100 for the liquidation of his expenses in transportation of his gear to that burgh, and in full of his bygone salaries from Whitsunday 1638 till Martinmas 1639. His son Andro succeeded him in Glasgow, but removed to Edinburgh about 1660, receiving sixty merks "to help to transport his guids and flitting to Edinburgh again," where he obtained the appointment of printer to the city and college. Andro Anderson printed a New Testament in Black letter for the use of children and schools; but this work had so many errors in it that the Privy Council in 1671 ordered all the copies to be called in and the blunders amended, and before it could be re-issued Anderson had to prefix a new title-page announcing the correction of the errors. Notwithstanding this grievous fault, "for payment of a composition in exchequer and other weighty reasons," Anderson soon after received a gift under the Great Seal, appointing him his Majesty's "sole, absolute, and only printer," and giving him the supervising of the presses and printing-houses in the kingdom,— a privilege so exclusive that no one dared print any book, from a Bible to a ballad, without license from Anderson. After his death in 1676, Agnes Campbell,

Campbell, widow of Andro Anderson, carried on the printing business under the same privileges, in company with some others who had apparently been in partnership with Anderson himself; but the company soon disagreed, as they thought themselves injured by the acting partners, and they all, with the exception of one George Swinton, sold their shares in the printing-house and patent to the widow, who thus became possessed of the monopoly of printing over all Scotland. Mrs. Anderson now began to prosecute the printers throughout the country for issuing books without her permission, and several were imprisoned and their places of business shut up. Swinton's share having been bought up by Robert Sanders, he assumed the title of one of the King's printers, and printed some books in an excellent manner, but he also was prosecuted. At length, John Reid, one of those against whom Mrs. Anderson had taken proceedings, petitioned the Duke of York in 1680 against the exclusiveness of her privilege, setting forth that she had endeavoured to keep him out of the trade, Mrs. Anderson maintaining that she had the sole right, and that "one press is sufficiently able to serve all Scotland, our printing being but inconsiderable." The matter being moved in the Privy Council, the Duke declared it could only be

the

the King's pleasure that his printer should enjoy those privileges which his royal predecessors had been in use to grant to their printers, such as printing of Bibles, Acts of Parliament, &c.; upon which the Privy Council allowed the printers to carry on their ordinary work, Mrs. Anderson's monopoly being limited to such works as had been specified in the gift to her husband's predecessor, Evan Tyler. Baffled by the printers, Mrs. Anderson now fell foul of the booksellers, and seized a quantity of Bibles brought by them from London; but they complained of this to the Council, and having printed the errata of one of her Bibles to justify their importing the books, after close debate the Council ordered the books to be returned.

In 1682, Sir Thomas Murray of Glendoick, having digested the statutes more carefully than had been done formerly, obtained liberty from Charles II. to employ in printing them those whom he might find most capable of executing so important a work. Sir Thomas having for this purpose contracted with David Lindsay, merchant in Edinburgh, and John Cairns, printer, a patent was made out, giving them the sole privilege of printing the Acts of Parliament for nineteen years. To execute the work, two tradesmen, named Joshua Van Solingen and Jan Colmar, as well as new printing

printing materials, were brought from Holland. Cairns dying, the Dutchmen acquired the property of the printing-house and published the Acts of Parliament in folio. As Mrs. Anderson, notwithstanding the check she had received from the Privy Council, harassed the Dutchmen in the exercise of their business, Lindsay obtained a patent from Charles II. for himself and his partners for printing any book which was not the peculiar privilege of the King's printer, and this patent shows that Anderson's monopoly had proved dishonourable to the King and disastrous to the country. The Dutchmen's business eventually fell into disorder, and they sold the printing-house to James Watson, merchant in Aberdeen, who had, in lieu of repayment of money lent by him to Charles II. when in exile, procured the gift of an exclusive privilege of printing almanacs in Scotland, and of the office of printer to his Majesty's household, with a salary of £100 a year; and for his son, a reversionary grant of the office of King's printer on the expiry of Anderson's patent. By the father's death, however, which happened some time after, it was neglected to get the patent to pass the seals.

"Nothing," says Watson's History, "came from the Royal Press (as Mrs. Anderson vainly termed it), but the most illegible and incorrect Bibles and books

books that ever were printed in any one place in the world. She regarded not the honour of the nation, and never minded the duty lay upon her as the sovereign's servant. Prentices, instead of the best workmen, were generally employed in printing the sacred word of God. And, in fine, nothing was studied but gaining of money by printing Bibles at any rate, which she knew none other durst do, and that nobody could want them." Many of the errata in Mrs. Anderson's Bibles were quite ungrammatical, and seriously affected the sense, as *righteousness* for *unrighteousness; he killed,* for *he is killed; for that have sinned,* for *for that all have sinned; enticed in every thing,* for *enriched in every thing; we* for *ye; either* for *neither; world* for *word; loveth pleasure,* for *liveth in pleasure; perfect* for *priest; thou hast slain,* for *thou wast slain; his testimony,* for *their testimony; of the flesh,* for *of the will of the flesh; ye were not the servants of sin,* for *ye were the servants of sin; be not better against them,* for *be not bitter against them.* Few pages can be opened in some of her Bibles without noticing such careless misspellings as *Tius* for *Titus, Timoty* for *Timothy;* and *the saints which are at Ephesus,* reads in one case *the saits which are at Epesus.* Again, in a quarto Bible, we have the following examples of carelessness in the metrical Psalms;

Psalms; as in Psalm xxv. 3, where the word *be*, which should conclude the first line of the verse, is carried down to the third—thus:

> "Yea, let thou none ashamed
> that do on thee attend:
> Ashamed let them be, O Lord, be
> who without cause offend."

In Psalm xliii. 5 we find

> "He of my count'nance is the *head*,"

instead of

> "He of my count'nance is the *health*."

In Psalm xix. 3 the words *to which* are omitted at the end of the first line, thus:

> "'There is no speech nor tongue
> their voice doth not extend."

In another Bible there are five columns in which the Italic *a* occurs 700 times for the Roman "a," exhausted in her fount of type; as in this verse, Gen. xxi. 14:

"*A*nd *A*braham rose up early in the morning, *a*nd took bread *a*nd *a* bottle of water, *a*nd gave *it* unto Hag*e*r (putting *it* on her shoulder) *a*nd the child *a*nd sent

sent her away: and she departed and wandered in the wilderness of Beer-sheba."

Another edition in 12mo, published in 1705, is printed in such a manner as might puzzle any reader not previously acquainted with the sacred text, and must have been incomprehensible to learners. Thus, what could be made of the sentence: Whyshoulditbethoug tathingincredi ble w'you, y' God should raise the dead?" The page from which these words are taken contains other errors. In the same year in which this Bible was published, Mrs. Anderson seems to have given offence by the price she charged for some of her books, and the Privy Council on November 20 found it necessary to interfere with her in this way also: "The Lords of Her Majesties Privie Counsell doe heirby appoynt and ordaine the Actis past in the last Session of Queen Ann's Parliament to be sold at one pund ten Shillings Scots, and discharges Mrs. Anderson, her Majesties Printer, to exact any more for the samen."

On February 26, 1685, the curious book, "Satan's Invisible World Discovered, by George Sinclair, professor of philosophy at the College of Glasgow," was endowed by the Lords of the Privy Council with a copyright of eleven years, all persons whatsoever being prohibited "from printing, reprinting,

reprinting, or importing into this kingdom, any copies of the said book," during that space of time. This little volume, which was often reprinted during the eighteenth century, contains, in the language of its own title-page, a "Choice Collection of Modern Relations, proving evidently against the *Saducees* and *Atheists* of this present age, that there are Devils, Spirits, Witches, and Apparitions, from authentic records and attestations of witnesses of undoubted verity." The Council also in June and September 1686 issued edicts against the selling of books reflecting on Popery, and sent their officer round the various booksellers to warn them. The following is a copy of one of these edicts: "Act prohibiteing the printing or reprinting of any New Books or Pamphletts, without License from the Lord High Chancellour, Sept. 7, 1686: The Lords of his Majesties Privy Councill Doe hereby Prohibite and Discharge all personis whatsomever from granting any license for printing or reprinting any new Books or Pamphletts, untill the same be first seen and perused by the Lord High Chancellor, as they will be answerable; And Ordaines Intimations hereof to be made by one of the Macers of Councill to the Printers and Stationers in and about Edinburgh, that they may not pretend ignorance. PERTH, *Cancell.*"

Amongst

Amongst others, the officer brought the edict to a bookseller named James Glen, who quietly observed that "there was one book in his shop which condemned Popery very directly, namely, the Bible,—might he sell that?" Some time after, when the Government were rigorously enforcing the laws against unlicensed printing, to prevent the issue of controversial pamphlets, James Glen was imprisoned by an order from the Chancellor, Lord Perth, for publishing a pamphlet called "The Root of Romish Ceremonies," designed "to prove Popery to be only paganism revived." This was considered a strong step for the Government to take at the time, when a Popish printer was at work at Holyrood; but perhaps Lord Perth—who had become a Catholic, "some say to please his wife, some to please the King, no one to please himself"—felt sore at the sharp answer Glen had given to the Council's officer on the former occasion, and thus was the more inclined to deal rigorously with him. Similar decrees, both permissive and restrictive, were afterwards at different times issued by the authorities to Robert Blaw and James Watson; and several are in existence referring to early newspapers, "Prognostications" or "Almanacks," and even to "Buriall Letters," respectively to Charles Chalmers in 1695, to James Donaldson

Donaldson and to George Mosman in 1699, and to various other printers and booksellers in 1703 and 1704, in which latter years there were several petitions to the Council regarding the restrictions on the art of printing.

CHAPTER VIII.

Watson, Symson, and Ruddiman.

AMONG the early printers who now follow, few names are of historical note, except those perhaps of James Watson, Andrew Symson, and Thomas Ruddiman. When the elder Watson came from Aberdeen, he set up his printing business somewhere in the Grassmarket, near Heriot's Hospital, but was evidently not successful, as we learn that in 1685-86 his landlady poinded his goods for rent due by him, and he took sanctuary within the precincts of Holyrood Abbey, taking his printing establishment with him. In all probability, it was at the time of the printer's indebtedness to his landlady that he made application for the repayment of his loan to Charles II.; but, as usual, the cash not being forthcoming, his improvident Majesty gave Watson the grant already referred to of printer to the Royal Family, with a privilege of printing Almanacks, or Prognostications, as they were then called. On the death

death of the elder Watson in 1687, his son James being then too young to succeed him, the office thus created was given by James VII. to Peter Bruce, or, as Watson calls him, "Bruschii," an engineer by trade and a German by birth. But Bruce did not make much by being so favoured, for though he got possession of the printing-house at Holyrood, and did some work there, he not long after was ruined by the rioters at the Revolution.

James Watson, bred a printer "from his infancy," as he himself says, and associated with his father at the Holyrood House press, set up in 1695, was, like the other printers of Edinburgh, very soon involved in trouble with Mrs. Anderson. A more serious difficulty awaited him, however, for he gave offence to the authorities by printing a pamphlet called "Scotland's Grievance respecting Darien," and he was apprehended and put in prison. Here he did not remain long, for on the 19th June 1700, a rumour having reached Edinburgh that the Spaniards had attacked the Scots colony at Darien and been signally defeated, these glad tidings raised such a tumult of rejoicing that a large mob assembled, kindled bonfires, and forced the citizens to illuminate their houses, breaking the windows of those who declined to similarly manifest their pleasure.

pleasure. The mob also forced its way into the house of Sir James Stewart, the King's Advocate, and compelled him to sign a warrant for liberating Watson, and also Paterson—the latter, no doubt, the projector of the Darien Scheme. While one portion of the mob was thus engaged, another body of rioters, more earnest and more zealous, without waiting for legal warrants, assaulted the prison, forced an entrance, and liberated Watson, Paterson, and other prisoners. Watson after this for a time prudently abstained from making any public appearance, till the general excitement had greatly abated; and Mrs. Anderson took the opportunity of Watson's partial retirement to again set the law in motion against him for infringing her monopoly, alleging also that he was a fugitive from justice, and had been educated a Papist, but for the purpose of carrying on his business professed to be a Protestant. She was so far successful on this occasion that she procured a warrant in 1701 to shut up Watson's workshop; but an appeal being made, Watson says, "On a full consideration of the case and debate before their Lordships, she was so well exposed that she made no attempt afterwards of that kind." Watson's first printing-house was in Warriston Close, but at this time it was in Craig's Close, opposite the Cross, where he had removed in 1697, and

and here he continued to print while he lived, the place being long known after his death as the King's Printing-House. He also opened a bookseller's shop in 1709, opposite the Luckenbooths, near to St. Giles's Church.

Attention has already been directed (p. 178) to the "Diurnal" reprinted by Higgins in 1652 at Leith; this was superseded by the "Mercurius Politicus," also at Leith, in 1653, and transferred to Edinburgh in November 1654, where it was published till 1660. Some numbers of "Mercurius Publicus" were republished in Scotland also in 1660, being succeeded by the "Kingdom's Intelligencer" in 1661, which continued till 1674. The first newspaper written as well as printed in Scotland, those previously named being all reprints of English origin, was the "Mercvrivs Caledonivs: Comprising the Affairs now in Agitation in Scotland. With a Survey of Forraign Intelligence." This small quarto, of varying extent, from 8 to 12, 14, or 16 pages, was begun in January 1660, and published weekly by "a society of Stationers," and edited by Thomas St. Serfe, or Tom Sydserfe, but only reached its twelfth number. No further effort seems to have been made to establish a native newspaper for nearly twenty years, when in December 1680 appeared the "Edinburgh Gazette," which also was

was very short-lived; but its title was revived in March 1699 by the first number of another "Gazette," a folio of two pages, edited by James Donaldson, and printed by James Watson in Craig's Close. The Privy Council Register throws some light on the history of this journal, and on the scanty measure of liberty then accorded to the press in the North.

"ACTS IN FAVORS OF JAMES DONALDSON FOR PRINTING THE GAZETTE.

[March 10, 1699.]

" Anent the petition given in to the Lords of his Majesties Privy Councill be James Donaldson merchant in Edinburgh, Shewing, That the petitioner doeth humbly conceive the publishing of ane Gazett in this place containeing ane abridgment of fforaigne newes togither with the occurrances at home may be both usefull and satisfieing to the leidges, and actually hath published one or two to see how it may be liked, and so farr as he could understand the project was approven of by very many, And therefore Humbly supplicating the saids Lords to the effect after mentioned; The Lords of his Majesties Privy Councill haveing considered this petition given in to them by the above James Donaldsone, They doe hereby Grant full warrand and authority to the petitioner for publishing the above Gazette, and Discharges any other persones whatsoever to pen or publish the

the like, under the penaltie of forfaulting all the coppies to the petitioner, and farder payment to him of the soume of ane hundred pounds Scots money, by and attour the forsaid confiscatioun and forfaulture, and Recommends to the Lord high Chancellor to nominat and appoint a particular persone to be Supervisor of the said Gazetts before they be exposed to publict view, printed, or sold."

Captain Donaldson, the projector of this paper—"writer of the Gazette" he called himself—began life as a merchant in Edinburgh. In 1689 he levied a company of foot at his own charge, and served in the Earl of Angus's regiment, until, on the termination of the Revolution wars, the strength of the regiment was reduced from twenty to thirteen companies. Donaldson was then turned adrift on the world—his business gone, his fortune spent—and it was in this strait that he conceived the idea of starting the Gazette, combining with his editorial labours the dolorous printing of funeral cards after a new fashion, "with the decencie and ornament of a border of skeletons, mortheads, and other emblems of mortality." The enterprise did not wholly answer his expectation, but he made shift to live thereby, till his fortunes were once more overcast by the appearance of the first number of "The Edinburgh Courant" in February 1705,

printed

printed also by James Watson, the printing of the "Gazette" having been transferred to John Reid. This first number is made up of extracts from the Paris and Amsterdam Gazettes and a "London-written" letter; the only local news being the following brief paragraphs :

"On Saturday last, Captain Green, Captain of the Ship Worchester, and the rest of his Crew who are Prisoners here, and are to be try'd as Pyrats, before the Judge-Admiral, has each of them got a Copy of their Inditement to answer against the 5th. of March next ; and the Lords of her Majesty's Privy-Council, has appointed five of their number to be Assessors to the Judge-Admiral.

"This day Robert Pringle one of the Tellers of the Bank, who lately went off with about 425 lib. sterling of the Bank's Money, is to be Try'd for Life before the Lords of Justiciary, upon a Lybel rais'd at the instance of the Treasurer of the Bank, and the said Pringle's Cautioners, with concourse of Her Majesty's Advocat.

"Leith, Feb. 16. This day came in to our Port the Mary Galley, David Preshu Commander, laden with Wine and Brandy."

There are also three advertisements, and two official notices regarding the paper itself. The advertisements refer to a sale of land, a post-office notice, and the third to some "Famous Loozengees for curing the Cold, stopping and pains in the Breast,

Breast, the Kinkhost," &c. "Price 8 sh. the Box."

Donaldson had interpreted the grant of the Privy Council given him in March 1699 as conferring a monopoly of the Edinburgh press; but the Lords of Council understood it differently, and did not hesitate to sanction the publication of the new journal as follows :

"ACT IN FAVOURS OF ADAM BOIG FOR PRINTING THE EDINBURGH CURRANT.

[Feb. 13. 1705.]

"Anent the petition given in and presented to the Lord high Chancellor and remanent Lords of Privie Councill By Adam Boig, Humbly Shewing, That wheras their petitioner intends to sett forth a paper by the name of Edinburgh Currant which will come out thrice weekly, viz. Monday, Wednesday, and Fryday, containing most of the remarkable forreign newes from their prints, and also the home newes from the ports within this Kingdome, when Ships comes and goes, and from whence, which its hoped will prove a great advantage to merchants and others within this Nation, (it being now altogether neglected); And Seeing their petitioner has no inclination to give offence therby to the Government, and that he cannot safely doe the same without he be empowered therto by their Lordships, And therfore craving to the effect after mentioned as the said petition bears ;

bears; The Lords of her Majesties Privie Councill having considered the above petition given in to them by Adam Boig, and the samen being read in their presence, The saids Lords doe heirby allow and grant warrand to the petitioner to sett furth and print ane paper entituled Edinburgh Currant, containing the remarkable forreign newes from their prints and letters, as also the home newes from the ports within this Kingdome, when Ships comes and goes, and from whence; he alwayes being answerable for the samen, and for the newes therin specified and sett doun."

Captain Donaldson strove hard against the new paper, complaining principally about its underselling him ; but it quickly made its way into favour, and soon began to push the " Gazette " from the field. Though strong in public support, the career of the new paper was not without its crosses, and before it was five months old it got into trouble with the authorities about what seems now an innocent enough advertisement from Evander M'Iver, manager of the " Scots Manufactory Paper-Mills." The Privy Council not only stopped the publication of the " Courant," but also of the " Gazette," though Donaldson states the advertisement did not appear there. The restriction of the " Gazette " lasted only a few weeks, that of the " Courant " extended to five months, and was removed only by by the editor subscribing a declaration, "That I shall publish nothing in my Courant concerning the Government till first the same be revised by the Clerks of Her Majesty's Privy Council." Boig died on the 27th June 1710—the last number which he edited being No. 685; and on the margin of a copy of this issue, preserved in the Advocates' Library, is written the words, "This day the Courantier dyed."

With Boig's death the Privy Council privilege took end, and though the paper continued to appear for a short time, it no longer bore to be "Published by Authority." At this time James Watson was engaged in printing the "Scots Courant," edited by James Muirhead, first begun in September 1705, and which Watson continued to issue till 1718. Boig's privilege was extended to another journal with the original name, edited by Daniel Defoe; but the editor having returned to London, the paper came under different management, requiring a consequent change of title to guard against any legal infringement, and it became known as the "Edinburgh Evening Courant"—a name it long continued to bear. The editor, James M'Ewen, obtained the exclusive privilege of the title, on the condition that "he be obliged before publication to give ane copy of his print to the Magistrates."

M'Ewen's

M'Ewen's paper appears to have been really a revival, in slightly altered form, of the original "Courant." It was published three times a week, and consisted of six pages. This paper finally relinquished publication in February 1886.

Besides the early newspapers already mentioned, there was the "Edinburgh Gazette," a new series in 4to, begun in 1706; the "Edinburgh Gazette," a third series in folio, begun in 1707; the "Scots Postman, or the New Edinburgh Gazette," established in 1708; the "Scots Postman," another series, begun in August 1709; the "Edinburgh Flying Post," commenced in October 1708; the "Northern Tatler," in April 1710; the "Examiner," in September 1710; the "Evening Post; or the New Edinburgh Gazette," in 1710; the "Edinburgh Gazette; or Scots Postman," in March 1715; the "Caledonian Mercury" having its re-birth, after an interval of sixty years, in April 1720, &c. Watson no doubt was connected with several of these papers, as well as the first "Gazette" and first "Courant," and one periodical with which he was connected in 1699 may be noted here. This was a monthly literary journal or magazine in the form of a small quarto of 56 pages, entitled "The History of the Works of the Learned; or, an Impartial Account of Books lately Printed in all parts

parts of Europe. With a particular Relation of the State of Learning in each country." The periodical contains reviews of recent books, with notices of others about to be printed. This, though only a reprint of a London publication, probably may have been the precursor of the "Scots Magazine," a periodical of like nature, begun in 1739.

In August 1711, on the approach of the expiry of Mrs. Anderson's patent, Watson, along with Robert Freebairn, another Edinburgh printer, and John Baskett, Queen's Printer for England, made an endeavour to secure the appointment of Royal Printers for Scotland, each of the three partners to have an equal share. This effort was successful, and the patent was made out in Freebairn's name for forty-one years, and passed the seals in October 1711. The malevolent spirit of Mrs. Anderson was again brought into play by this, and working on the avarice of Freebairn, she endeavoured to exclude Watson from his third share in the patent, and herself become a partner in the company. A lawsuit arose in consequence, which, after considerable delay, was decided by the Court of Session in June 1715 in Watson's favour. It was at this time, while the lawsuit was pending, that Watson brought out his "History of Printing," to which reference has already been made, a small
sixpenny

sixpenny pamphlet of 64 pages, which contains very little history, but much scolding of Mrs. Anderson, as well as specimens of the various kinds of type Watson then possessed. At the end of the little book there occurs the following curious poem on the art of printing:

A CONTEMPLATION

UPON THE MYSTERY OF MAN'S REGENERATION, IN ALLUSION TO THE MYSTERY OF PRINTING.

GREAT Bleſt MASTER-PRINTER, *Come*
Into thy Compoſing-Room:
Wipe away our foul Offences;
Make, O make our Souls and Senſes,
 The Upper *and the* Lower Caſes;
And thy large Alphabet *of Graces*
The Letter, *which being ever fit,*
O haſte thou to Diſtribute *it:*
For there is (I make Account)
No Imperfection *in the* Fount.
If any Letters Face *be* foul,
O waſh *it, ere it touch the Soul;*
Contrition be the Bruſh; *the* Lye,
Tears from a Penitential Eye.
 Thy Graces ſo Diſtributed,
Think not thy Work half finiſhed:
On ſtill, O LORD, no Time defer,
Be truly a COMPOSITER.

Take

Take thy Compoſing-Stick *in Hand,*
Thy Holy Word, the firmeſt Band;
For ſure that Work can never miſs,
That's truly Juſtify'd *in this.*

　The End of Grace's Diſtribution,
Is not a meer Diſſolution;
But that from each Part being cited,
They may be again United:
Let Righteouſneſs and Peace then meet,
Mercy and Truth each other greet;
Let theſe Letters *make a* Word,
Let theſe Words *a* Line *afford,*
Then of Lines *a* Page compoſe,
Which being brought unto a Cloſe,
Be Thou the Direction, *L O R D;*
Let Love be the faſt-binding Cord.
Set, *O L O R D, O* Set *apace,*
That we may grow from Grace to Grace;
Till tow'rds the Chace *we nearer draw,*
The Two ſtrong Tables of Thy Law,
Of which the Two *firm* Croſſes *be,*
The Love of Man, next after Thee.
The Head-Sticks *are Thy Majeſty;*
The Foot-Sticks, *Chriſt's Humility;*
The Supplications of the Saints,
The Side-Sticks, *when our Faith e'er faints;*
Let the Quines *be Thy ſure Election,*
Which admits of no Rejection;
With which our Souls being join'd about,
Not the leaſt Grace can drop out.
Thy Mercies and Allurements all,
Thy Shooting-Stick *and* Mallet *call.*

　　　　　　　　　　　　　　　　But

But when all this done we see,
Who shall the CORRECTOR be?
O LORD, What Thou Set'st cann't be ill,
It needs then no CORRECTOR's Skill.

Now tho' these Graces all are Set,
Our Hearts are but White-Paper yet;
And by Adam's First Transgression,
Fit only for the worst Impression.
Thy Holy Spirit the PRESS-MAN make
From whom we may Perfection take;
And let Him no Time defer,
To Print on us Thy Character.
Let the Ink be Black as Jet;
What though? It is comely yet,
As Courtains of King Solomon,
Or Kedars Tents to look upon.

Be Victory the Press's Head,
That o'er Oppression it may tread.
Let Divine Contemplation be
The Skrews, to raise us up to Thee:
The Press's Two Cheeks (unsubdu'd)
Strong Constancy and Fortitude:
Our slavish Flesh let be the Till,
Whereon lay what Trash you will:
The Nut and Spindle, Gentleness,
To move the Work with Easiness:
The Platten is Affliction,
Which makes good Work, being hard set on.
The Bar, the Spirit's Instrument,
To sanctifie our Punishment.
The Blankets, a Resemblance hath
Of Mercy in the midst of Wrath.

The

The Frisket, *thy Preventing Grace,*
Keeps us from many a fully'd Face.
CHRIST JESUS is the Level Stone
That our Hearts must be Wrought *upon.*
The Coffin, *wherein it doth ly,*
Is Rest to all Eternity.
The Cramp-Irons, *that it moves on still,*
Are the good Motions of the Will.
The Rounce, *the Spirit's Inspiration,*
Working an Holy Agitation.
The Girts, *the Gift of Continence,*
The Tether of th' Unbridled Sense.
The Winter, *whereon all doth ly,*
Is Patience in Adversity.
The Footstep, *Humbleness of Mind,*
That in it self no Worth can find.

 If there be such a Chance as this,
That any Letter *batter'd is,*
Being come unto thy View,
Take *it out, put in a new.*
Or if Satan, that foul Fiend,
Marr, with a Pretence to Mend,
And being at thy Goodness vext,
Makes Blasphemy of thy pure Text,
Find it out, O LORD, and then
Print our Hearts new o'er agen.

 O LORD, unto this Work make hast,
'Tis a Work that long will last:
And when this White-Paper's *done,*
Work a Reiteration.

The above lines are evidently not original in
Watson's

Watson's book, for they are also found amongst the scraps collected by John Bagford early in the eighteenth century for a History of Printing, and which are now among the Harleian MSS. in the British Museum. Bagford introduces his manuscript with these remarks: "The following Poem, written many years ago, and now quite out of print, I have added to this paper, being very well assured it will be very acceptable to all lovers of the noble mystery of Printing." From its style, he says, it appears to be of the time of Cromwell.

On the breaking out of the Rebellion of 1715, Freebairn joined the cause of James Stuart, and set off for Perth, to act as printer to the Pretender. This step led to his forfeiture, and Mrs. Anderson and Baskett applied for and received a new patent; but singularly enough, notwithstanding his overt act of rebellion, on taking proceedings against the new patentees, Freebairn recovered his rights, and King George continued to employ him and his assignees as printers till 1752. Watson's rights, which of course had been imperilled by his partner's proceedings, were also re-confirmed by the same judgment of the Court.

In Watson's hands the art of printing recovered much of the credit it had recently lost through the negligent methods pursued by Mrs. Anderson and others,

others, and he is said to have brought over from the Continent the best materials and the best workmen he could procure; but it was in the printing of the Bible that he excelled. His small Bibles of 1715, 1716, 1719, and especially his folio Bible of 1722, occupy an honourable place for excellent workmanship and accuracy. One book of Watson's claims particular notice here—his well-known collection of Scots Poems, "comprised of such Poems as have been formerly Printed most Uncorrectly, in all respects, but are now copied from the most Correct Manuscripts that could be procured of them." This work preserved many most interesting specimens of our ancient vernacular poetry.* It is gratifying to learn that, notwithstanding all his difficulties and troubles, fortune seems to have smiled upon him. He died on 24th September 1722, and was buried in Greyfriars Churchyard. Watson's rights in the patent were assigned to John Mosman and William Brown, but it is said "they did not walk in his footsteps by seeking to maintain the reputation he left them."

Andrew Symson, about 1700, was a most worthy successor,

---

* Originally published by Watson in Three Parts, a very fine reprint in one volume was issued by Messrs. Ogle and Co. of Glasgow in 1869.

successor, whose printing-press was in a range of buildings in Cowgate, between the foot of College and Horse Wynds. He was a man of learning, having received a University education, and at one time was Episcopal curate of Kirkinner in Galloway, but was ousted from his charge at the Revolution. While minister or curate of Kirkinner, he wrote the "Large Description of Galloway," 1684. "He was a man of rare Christian charity. Though his congregation dwindled down to three persons, he would give no information to the Government as to the recusant Covenanters who formed the bulk of his parishioners. In 1688, when the ecclesiastical pendulum swung to the opposite extreme of the arc, and Presbyterianism again became the established religion of Scotland," he was "necessitate to retire to a quiet lurking-place."

On his establishment as a printer in Edinburgh, Symson combined the art of printing with the writing of books, and published a lengthy poem of his own, which is stated in the preface as "issued from my printing-house at the foot of Horse Wynd, in the Cowgate, February 16, 1705." It is entitled "Tripatriarchion; or the Lives of the Three Patriarchs, Abraham, Isaac, and Jacob, executed forth of the sacred story, and digested into English verse." Before Symson issued this work, he had edited

edited and published an edition of the "Laws and Customs of Scotland," by the well-known Lord Advocate, Sir George Mackenzie, which bears on its title-page, "Printed by the heirs and successors of Mr. Andrew Anderson, printer to the King's most excellent Majesty, for Mr. Andrew Symson, and are to be sold by him in the Cowgate, near the foot of Horse Wynd, Anno Dom. 1699." An elegantly bound copy of this work is in the Advocates' Library.

Thomas Ruddiman, a distinguished grammarian, scholar, and printer, was born in Banffshire in October 1674, and received his education in the parish school and at King's College, Aberdeen. In June 1694 he took the degree of M.A., and in February 1695 was appointed schoolmaster of Laurencekirk in Kincardineshire, where he remained three years and a half. About the end of 1699, the celebrated Dr. Pitcairn invited him to Edinburgh with the promise of his patronage. Ruddiman accordingly repaired to the metropolis in 1700, and on his arrival procured employment in the Advocates' Library, where he was in May 1702 appointed assistant librarian. He contrived to augment the small income derived from this source by revising and editing works for the booksellers, his first publication of this kind being Sir Robert Sibbald's "Introductio

"Introductio ad Historiam Rerum a Romanis Gestarum in ea Boreali Britanniæ parte quæ ultra Murum Picticum est." In 1707 Ruddiman commenced practising as book auctioneer, confining himself principally to the sale of learned works and school-books. In connection with this it may be interesting to notice that the first sale of books by auction which ever took place in Scotland was at Edinburgh about the end of 1688. The announcement was made by Andrew Anderson, and was in the following very explicit terms: "A catalogue of excellent and rare books, especially histories and romances, for the most part in English, and the variorums, are to be sold by way of auction, the twelfth day of November 1688. The books are to be seen from the first day of November to the day of auction at Edinburgh, on the south side of the High Street, a little above the Cross, being the close immediately above the Fishmarket Close, in the head of the said close, on the left hand, where a *placat* will be on the gate, and the catalogues are to be had there *gratis*. The time for the sale is only in the afternoon, from two of the clock till four. Edinburgh, printed in the year 1688. He who pays not his money presently, is to give earnest, to take them away and pay his money before the next day of the auction begins; or else to lose his earnest,

THOMAS RUDDIMAN.

earnest, and the books to be put to sale again. What books shall happen to be unsold at the auction, are to be had afterwards."

Ruddiman in 1711 aided in preparing for publication a new edition of the works of Drummond of Hawthornden, and assisted Abercromby with the first volume of his "Martial Achievements of the Scots' Nation." In 1713, on the death of his friend Dr. Pitcairn, in his character of auctioneer, Ruddiman managed the sale of his library, which was purchased by Peter the Great, Emperor of Russia. In 1714 he published his "Rudiments of the Latin Tongue," which at once superseded every work of a similar nature, and continued long to be the standard elementary class-book for the Latin language in the schools of Scotland. His valuable edition of the works of Buchanan, with notes, in folio, appeared in 1715, in which year he also began printing, in partnership with his brother Walter, who had been brought up to the business; the first production of their press being the second volume of Abercromby's "Martial Achievements."

Ruddiman began to print the "Caledonian Mercury" in 1724, afterwards acquiring the whole property of that newspaper, which continued in his family till 1772, when it was sold by the trustees of his grandchildren. He became afterwards, conjunctly

junctly with James Davidson, printer to the University, and in 1730, on the death of John Spottiswood, was appointed principal librarian to the Advocates' Library.

During the summer of 1745, Ruddiman retired from the disturbed scenes of Edinburgh to the sequestered quiet of the country, and afterwards issued several small treatises on disputed parts of Scottish history. He also contributed assistance to various works, and printed many of the classics, which are still sought after and prized. In 1751, when at the age of seventy-seven, his eyesight began to fail, but this did not prevent him from continuing his correspondence with his friends or pursuing his studies, and in the course of the same year he brought out an edition of Livy, in four volumes 12mo, which is said to be one of the most accurate ever published. He resigned his post of librarian on January 7, 1752, and was succeeded by David Hume. Ruddiman died at Edinburgh, January 19, 1757, aged eighty-three, and was interred in the Greyfriars Churchyard, where a monument was erected in 1806 to his memory.

The story of the Bassandyne Bible and the early typographers of Edinburgh may end here. Printers now become many, and the printing of Bibles

Bibles and their importation from England assumes such proportions as to render the further history of the subject only of ordinary interest, though the early history of the art of printing in Scotland is a fertile topic of social importance, requiring and deserving fuller treatment than it has as yet received.

To avoid encumbering the foregoing pages too much with footnotes, the principal authorities from which the information has been derived are here stated:

Tymperley's Encyclopædia of Typographical Anecdote.
Maitland Miscellany.
Maitland's Edinburgh.
Laing's Adversaria.
Leland's Collectanea.
Dibdin's Library Companion.
Nicol's Diary of Public Transactions (1650-1667).
Dibdin's Typographical Antiquities.
Mackenzie's History of Scotland.
Peterkin's Book of the Universall Kirk.
Calderwood's History of the Kirk of Scotland.
Beloe's Anecdotes of Literature.
Spottiswood's Miscellany, vol. i.
Watson's Scots Poems.
Watson's History of Printing.
Hansard's Typographia.
Laing's History of Scotland.
Westcott's General View of History of English Bible.
Dr. Eadie's External and Critical History of English Bible.
Dr. Eadie's Biblical Cyclopædia.
Dr. Lee's Memorial for Bible Societies.
Anderson's Annals of English Bible.
Dickson's "Who was Scotland's First Printer?"
Chambers's Domestic Annals of Scotland.

M'Crie's Life of John Knox.
Dunbar's Life and Poems.
Knox and his Times.
Records of the Church of Scotland.
Arnot's History of Edinburgh.
Anderson's Annals of Edinburgh.
Heron's History of Scotland.
Spalding's Troubles in Scotland.
Crawford's Scotland.
Tytler's History of Scotland.
Lockhart's History of Affairs in Scotland.
Abercromby's Scots Nation.
Memorials of Stuart Dynasty.
Pitcairn's Criminal Trials.
Aikman's Annals of the Persecution.
Pitscottie's Chronicles, &c. &c.

INDEX.

INDEX.

ABERDEEN Breviary, the, 73, 74, 76
Acts of Scottish Parliament, 17, 18, 27, 28, 34-36, 82-84, 89, 93, 95
Aldus, the printer, 40
Ales, Alexander, 26, 27
Anderson, Andro, 183; receives monopoly of printing, 184
Anderson, Mrs., 184; strong endeavours to repress all other printers, 185; limitation of the monopoly, 186; careless work done by, 186-188; errata in her Bibles, 188-190; contentions against James Watson, 196, 203
"Ane Fruitfull Meditation," 159
Arbuthnot, Alexander, 104; appeals to General Assembly regarding printing of Bible, 104-112; licensed to print Bible, 114; publication of Bible by, 119; appointed King's Printer, 119; curious result of his appointment, 122; death of, 125
Arbuthnot, Principal, 125

Archbishop of Canterbury's Bibles, 170, 171
Arran, Regent, 34-37
Auction of books, first, 214
Authorised Version, first edition of, in Scotland, 170
"Avowis of Alexander," the, 124

BASKETT, John, 205
Bassandyne Bible, the, proposal to print, 104; General Assembly sanctions printing of, 108; Privy Council license for, 114; publication of, 119; enforced sale of, 121; general title of, 126; type used in, 129; prefatory matter, 131, 132; the illustrations, 133; the "arguments," 134; marginal notes, 138; passages from, 141-155; appendices, &c., 155-157
Bassandyne, Thomas, 101; censured by General Assembly, 102; proposal to print Bible, 104-111; licensed to print Bible, 114; death of, 116
Beaton, Cardinal, 24, 25; attempts

to gain Regency, 34; condemns Wishart, 37; assassination of, 37
Bellenden's "History and Croniklis," 84
Bible, clandestine importation of the, 18, 19, 26; opposition to, 27; Bill to permit reading of, 35; in MS., 39; the Mazarin, 40; Tyndale's, 42-48; burning the, 50-52; Coverdale's, 55-57; Matthews', 57, 58; the Great, 58; chained in churches, 59-61; edict against the, in England, 63, 64; the Genevan, 65-68; first official license to print the, 96; proposal to General Assembly to print the, 104-112; license for first Scottish, 114; publication of first Scottish, 116-119; enforced sale of, 121, 122; collation of first Scottish or Bassandyne, 126-157; the "Whig," 133; the "Breeches," 133; Hart's editions of the, 163-165; first edition of Authorised Version in Scotland, 170; the Archbishop of Canterbury's, 170, 171; Tyler's editions of the, 177; Anderson's faulty editions of the, 184-190; Watson's editions of the, 211
Bill, Charles, 177
Blaw, Robert, 192
Blunders in Anderson's Bibles, 184

Blunders in Geneva Bible, 133
Bodley, Sir Thomas, 66
Boig, Adam, 201-203
Bonner, Bishop, 59, 63
Book of Common Prayer, 171
"Book of Godlie and Spirituall Sangs," 166
Books, first sale by auction of, 214
Books of religion, 18
Books, taxing imported, 161-163
"Breeches" Bible, the, 133
Breviarium Aberdonense, the, 73, 74
"Bruce," Barbour's, 166
Bruce, Peter, 195
Bryson, James, 175, 181
Bryson, Robert, 181, 182
Buchanan's History, 125
Buckenham, Dr., 20
"Buik of Alexander the Great," 124
Burning the Bible, 50-52
Burton, Hill, 74
Byddell, John, 85

CAIRNS, John, 186
"Caledonian Mercury," the, 204, 217
Campbell, Alexander, 24
Carron, William, 183
"Catechisme," Hamilton's, 87, 88
"Certane Tractatis," Winzet's, 92
Chained Bible, the, 59-61
Chalmers, George, 88, 125

Chambers, Dr. Robert, 78
Charles I., King, attempts to introduce Episcopal service, 172-176
Charteris, Henrie, 93, 124, 158-160
Charteris, Robert, 165
Chepman, Walter, 71; his device, 73, 74; his printing-house, 78; bequests to the Church, 79, 80
Chronicle, Halle's, 49-52
"Colloquies of Corderius," the, 160
Colmar, Jan, 186
"Complaynte and Testament," Lyndsay's, 85
"Complaynte of Scotland," the, 86
"Confessione of the Fayth," the, 94
Constantine, a heretic, 51, 52
Continental printing for Scotland, 160
Corruptions of the Church, 32, 33
Coverdale, Miles, 55; version of the Bible, 56, 57; exiled, 65
Cranmer's Bible, 58

DALGLEISH, George, 102
Darien Riot, the, 195, 196
Davidson, Thomas, 81; type used by, 82; license to, 82, 83; works printed by, 83-85
"Declaration concerning the Tumults in Scotland," 172

Dedication of Bassandyne Bible, 119
Dedications, Bible, 66
Device, the, of Chepman, 74; of Androw Myllar, 77; of John Scott, 87
"Dialog," Lyndsay's, 29
Discussion of opinions forbidden, 27
Donaldson, Captain James, 198; licensed to print "Gazette," 198; previous career, 199; petitions against "Courant," 202; his Gazette suspended, 202
"Donat," the, 97
Dunbar Rudiments, the, 140
Dunbar, William, 69, 75, 80
"Diurnal of some Passages of Affairs," 178, 197

EARLY Scottish newspapers, 199-204
Edicts against books reflecting on Popery, 191, 192
Edicts against the Bible, 17, 18, 63, 64
Edicts against unlicensed printing, 98
"Edinburgh Courant," the, 199; the first number, 200; Lords of Council license, 201; suspension of the paper, 202; restriction removed, 203; death of Boig, the "Courantier," and consequent stoppage of publication, 203; revival under name of "Edinburgh

Evening Courant," 203; final relinquishment of publication, 204
"Edinburgh Flying Post," 204
"Edinburgh Gazette," the, 197, 204
Edward VI., King, 60
Egenolph, Christian, 56
Erasmus, Greek Testament of, 41
Errol, Earl of, 34
"Evening Post," the, 204
"Examiner," the, 204
Expositio Sequentiarium, the, 78, 79

"FALL of the Roman Kirk," the, 102
Finlayson, Thomas, 168, 169
Forrest, Henry, 24
Freebairn, Robert, appointed royal printer, 205; joins Pretender in 1715, 210
Froude, Mr., on Tyndale, 46
Fryth, John, 53

"GAZETTE," the, 198
General Assembly, the, jealous of the art of printing, 93; censures Bassandyne, 102; sanctions printing of Bible, 104-108; dedication by, of first Scottish Bible, 119; interference of, with the printers, 122
Geneva Bible, the, 65-68
Geneva, exiles at, 65
Gibson, John, 160, 161

Glencairn, Earl of, 34
Glen, James, 192
"God and the King," 168
Gourlaw, Robert, 124
Gourlay, John, the "customer," 162, 163
Great Bible, the, 58
Greek Testament of Erasmus, 41
"Gude and Godlie Ba'lats," 120
"Gushing Tears of Godly Sorrow," the, 182

HACKETT, John, 18, 48
Hamilton, Archbishop, 87, 88
Hamilton, Patrick, birth and education of, 21; flight to Germany, 22; at Marburg, 23; martyrdom of, 24; excitement caused by death of, 25
Hart, Andro, 160, 161; petition against taxing import of books, 161-163; high estimation of his work, 165; important works printed by, 166-168
Henry VIII., King, 60
Heres, Peter Groot, 112
Higgins, Christopher, 178, 197
History of Printing, Watson's, 171, 177, 205-210
"History of the Works of the Learned," 204
Hostingue, Laurence, 78
Hyslop, Archibald, 183

IGNORANCE of Roman Catholic clergy, 28, 32

Inscriptions on church walls, 63, 64
"Interpretation," the, of Garland, 78

JAMES IV., King, 69-73, 80
James V., King, 82, 83
James VI., King, 99, 112, 122, 123, 140, 159, 172
Joye, the Reformer, 52

KERKNETT, Salomon, "composer," 112, 116
Kilmaurs, Lord, 34
"Kingdom's Intelligencer," the, 197
"Kittie's Confession," Lyndsay's, 32
Knox, John, 36, 38

LAING, Dr., 76, 79, 124
"Last Blast," Winzet's, 91, 92
Laud, Archbishop, 172
"Laws and Customs of Scotland," Sir George Mackenzie's, 213
Lekprevik, Robert, 94; licensed to print Acts of Parliament, 95; to print "Inglis Bibill," 96; removal to St. Andrews, 97; falls into disgrace, 100
License to print Bible, first, 96
Lindsay, David, 186, 187
Lithgow, William, 182
Liturgy, attempted introduction of the, 173; consequent tumults, 173-176
Living, John, 65

"Logarithmorum," Napier's, 166
"Lustie Maye," 86
Lutheran doctrines in Scotland, 17
Luther, the Reformer, 45
Lyndsay, Sir David, 29-33, 69, 85, 90, 93

M'EWEN, James, 203
Mackenzie, Sir George, 213
Manuscript Bibles, 39
"Martial Achievements of Scots Nation," the, 217
Martyrdom of Patrick Hamilton and Forrest, 24; of George Wishart, 37; of William Tyndale, 54; of Rogers, 57, 58
Mary, Queen, of England, 63
Matthews' Bible, 57, 58
Maxwell, Lord, 34; introduces Bill for free Bible, 35, 36
Mazarin Bible, the, 40
"Mercvrivs Caledonivs," the, 197
"Mercurius Politicus," the, 197
"Mercurius Publicus," the, 197
Metrical Ballads, the, 75, 76
Monopoly of printing, Anderson's, 184
More, Sir Thomas, 52
Morton, Regent, 97-100, 116
Mosman, George, 193
Muirhead, James, 203
Murray of Glendoick, Sir Thomas, 186
Myllar, Androw, 70, 71; his device, 77; at Rouen, 78; his printing-house, 78-80

"Mystery of Man's Regeneration," the, 205-209

NAPIER'S "Logarithmorum," 166
National Covenant, the, 175
"New Edinburgh Gazette," the, 204
Newspapers, early Scottish, 199-204
New Testament, Tyndale's, 22, 55; the Greek, 40; the Genevan, 65
New Testamenters, the, 25, 28, 120
"Northern Tatler," the, 204
Norton, John, 161; petitions against imported books being taxed, 162, 163

"OFFICE of Our Lady of Pity," the, 81
Old Testament in Hebrew, the, 40

PAKINGTON, Augustus, 48-50
Paper-making in Scotland, 112, 113
Patent, Chepman and Myllar's, 71, 72
Paterson, projector of Darien Scheme, 196
Perth, Lord Chancellor, 192
Pitcairn, Dr., 213, 217
"Porteous of Noblenes," the, 73, 75, 76
"Practice of Prelates," the, 53
Printing, discovery of the art of, 40; introduction into Edinburgh, 69; patent permitting in Edinburgh, 71; Chepman and Myllar, 71-73; the Aberdeen Breviary, 73, 74; Metrical Romances, 75, 76; Myllar at Rouen, 78; Chepman's bequests to the Church, 79, 80; John Story, 81; Thomas Davidson, 81-84; royal license for printing parliamentary papers, 82, 83; Johne Skot, 85; the "Complaynte of Scotland," 86; Hamilton's Catechisme, 87; edict against printers, 89; aid of the art in diffusing liberal opinions, 93; Robert Lekprevik, 94; license to print "Inglis Bibill," 96; edict against unlicensed, 98; Bassandyne and Arbuthnot, 101-122; on the Continent, 160; Andro Hart, 161-168; Thomas Finlayson, 168, 169; Robert Young, 168-172; Evan Tyler, 177-181; Andro Anderson, 183; Mrs. Anderson, 184; deterioration of the art of, 187-190; edicts against unlicensed, 191-193; James Watson, 194; the early Scottish newspapers, 197-204; curious poem on the art of, 206-209; revival and progress of the art under Watson, 210, 211; Andrew Symson, 211-213; Thomas Ruddiman, 213-218

Prognostications or Almanacks, 192, 194

RABAN, printer in Aberdeen, 175
Ramsay, Andrew, 173
Ramsay, Patrick, 178
Reformation, causes promoting the, 29-33
Reformers, the exiled, 65
"Regiam Majestatem," Skene's, 169
Reid, John, 185, 200
"Remonstrance," Dunbar's, 80
"Remonstrance," the Covenanters', 175
Rogers, John, 57
Rollock, Henry, 173
Romish clergy, ignorance of, 28, 32
"Root of Romish Ceremonies," the, 192
Ros, John, 158
Rous, Francis, 182
Ruddiman, Thomas, 213-218
"Rudiments of Latin Tongue," 217
Ruthven, Lord, 34

ST. ANDREWS, importation of Bibles into, 19; martyrdom of Hamilton at, 24, 25; assassination of Beaton at, 37
St. Giles's Church, Chepman's chaplainries at, 79, 80
"Satan's Invisible World Discovered," 190

Scotch Psalms, the, 177, 182
"Scotland's Grievance respecting Darien," 195
Scots Manufactory Paper Mills, the, 202
"Scots Poems," Watson's, 211
"Scots Postman," the, 204
Scott, William, 98, 99
Seaton, Alexander, 25
"Seven Sages," the, 159, 160
Skene's, Lord, "Regiam Majestatem," 169
Skot, Johne, 85-93
Smith, Robert, 158
Solingen, Joshua van, 186
Spilman, John, 114
Stafford, Thomas, 163
Stewart, Sir James, 196
Story, John, 81
Swinton, George, 185
Sydserfe, Tom, 197
Symson, Andrew, 211-213
Synod, last Roman Catholic, 31
Synod of St. Andrews, 165

TATE, John, 113
Taxing imported books, 161-163
Tonstal, Bishop, 21, 41, 42, 48-50, 52, 59
"Tragedie," Lyndsay's, 90
"Tripatriarchion," Symson's, 212
Tulchan Bishops, 173
Tumults in Scotland concerning Liturgy, 172-176
Turnbull, Walter, 98, 99
"Twopenny Faith," the, 88, 89

Tyler, Evan, appointed royal printer, 177; joins Cromwell's party, 178; restored to his office, 181

Tyndale, William, 26, 27; education and character, 41; exile, 42; translates New Testament, 42; the Old Testament, 45; style and writing, 45, 46; peculiar genius of, 46; his interview with Pakington, 49, 50; his "Practice of Prelates," 53; martyrdom of, 54

Type, in Metrical Ballads, 75; in Aberdeen Breviary, 76; used by Hostingue, 78; used by Story, 81; used by Davidson, 82; in Bassandyne Bible, 129; Greek and Hebrew, 129, 130

VAUTROLLIER, Thomas, 123, 124, 158, 162

Vilvorde, martyrdom of Tyndale at, 54

WALDEGRAVE, Robert, 158

Watson, James, 194; imprisoned for printing pamphlet concerning Darien Scheme, 195; released by riotous mob, 196; Mrs. Anderson attempts to close his printing-house, 196; his bookseller's shop, 197; prints the "Gazette," 198; the "Courant," 200; prints the "Scots Courant," and other papers, 203, 204; applies for appointment of royal printer, 205; lawsuit against Mrs. Anderson, 205, 206; his History of Printing, 205–210; revival of the art under, 210; his editions of the Bible, 211; death of, 211

Wedderburn, James, 86, 166

"Whig" Bible, the, 133

Williamson, John, 121

Winzet, Niniane, 91, 92

Wishart, George, martyrdom of, 37

YOUNG, George, 159

Young, Robert, 168; printer to Charles I., 170; meritorious work done by, 171

York, Duke of, 185

THE END.

PRINTED BY BALLANTYNE, HANSON AND CO.
EDINBURGH AND LONDON.

www.ingramcontent.com/pod-product-compliance
Lightning Source LLC
Chambersburg PA
CBHW021819230426
43669CB00008B/798